EVERYONE COMMUNICATES,
FEW CONNECT

BRIAN,
THANKS FOR A
SUCCESSFUL 2012!
I WISH YOU THE
BEST IN 2013...

—KEN
12/12

EVERYONE COMMUNICATES, FEW CONNECT

WHAT THE MOST EFFECTIVE PEOPLE DO DIFFERENTLY

JOHN C. MAXWELL

THOMAS NELSON
Since 1798

NASHVILLE   DALLAS   MEXICO CITY   RIO DE JANEIRO

Published in Nashville, Tennessee, by Thomas Nelson. Thomas Nelson is a registered trademark of Thomas Nelson, Inc.

Published in association with Yates & Yates, www.yates2.com.

Thomas Nelson, Inc. titles may be purchased in bulk for educational, business, fund-raising, or sales promotional use. For information, please e-mail SpecialMarkets@ThomasNelson.com.

Scripture quotations from *The Message* by Eugene H. Peterson. © 1993, 1994, 1995, 1996, 2000. Used by permission of NavPress Publishing Group. All rights reserved.

Scripture quotations from HOLY BIBLE: NEW INTERNATIONAL VERSION®. © 1973, 1978, 1984, by International Bible Society. Used by permission of Zondervan Publishing House. All rights reserved.

Page 27 Cartoon © Randy Glasbergen.
Photographs were submitted by commentators on Dr. Maxwell's blog. Used by permission.

Library of Congress Cataloging-in-Publication Data

Maxwell, John C.
    Everyone communicates, few connect : what the most effective people do differently / John C. Maxwell.
        p. cm.
    Includes bibliographical references.
    ISBN 978-0-7852-1425-0
    ISBN 978-1-4002-8080-3 (IE)
    1. Business communication. 2. Interpersonal communication. 3. Interpersonal relations. I. Title.
    HF5718.M387 2009
    650.1'3—dc22

2009051528

Printed in the United States of America
11 12 13 14   QG   14 13 12

This book is dedicated to James Wesley Maxwell,
our fifth grandchild. He has already "connected" with his
Mimi and Papa. As he grows older, it is our prayer that
he will learn to connect effectively with others.

This book is dedicated to James Wesley Maxwell,
our fifth grandchild. He has already "connected" with his
Mimi and Papa. As he grows older, it is our prayer that
he will learn to connect effectively with others.

CONTENTS

CONTENTS

Acknowledgments

Thank you to
Charlie Wetzel, my writer
Stephanie Wetzel, my social media manager
and blog administrator
Sue Caldwell, who types the first draft
Linda Eggers, my assistant

And thank you to
the hundreds of people who
read the manuscript on
JohnMaxwellonLeadership.com
and gave me their feedback
(and whose names are listed beginning on page 251).

PROLOGUE

Last month I received an overseas phone call from Sangeeth Varghese, author, columnist, and founder of LeadCap, an organization developing leaders in India. He was interviewing me for *Forbes*. I enjoyed talking to Sangeeth, but we had a problem. Our phone connection was bad. I bet we got disconnected nearly a dozen times. One minute we'd be enjoying our conversation on leadership, and the next minute the line would go dead.

Everybody's had that happen during a phone call. It's the reason Verizon did their "Can you hear me now?" campaign. When your phone drops a call, you know it, don't you? And what is your reaction? How does it make you feel? Annoyed? Frustrated? Angry?

Have you ever thought about why you react the way you do when you get disconnected? Being disconnected wastes your time. It interrupts the flow of what you're trying to accomplish, and it undermines your productivity. The bottom line is that connecting is everything when it comes to communication.

You know when you don't have a good connection on the phone, but how about when you're communicating with people in person? Do you know when a connection has been made? Can you tell when the connection is starting to go bad? Can you identify when the "call" has been dropped?

Most people have an easy time knowing when the connection is good on the phone. But they have no idea if they're connecting with others in other everyday situations.

How do I tell? How do I know that I've connected with others? I look for the signs. When I interact with people, whether one on one, in a group, or with an audience, I know I've connected when I sense:

- EXTRA EFFORT—people go the extra mile

- UNSOLICITED APPRECIATION—they say positive things

- UNGUARDED OPENNESS—they demonstrate trust

- INCREASED COMMUNICATION—they express themselves more readily

- ENJOYABLE EXPERIENCES—they feel good about what they're doing

- EMOTIONAL BONDEDNESS—they display a connection on an emotional level

- POSITIVE ENERGY—their emotional "batteries" are charged by being together

- GROWING SYNERGY—their effectiveness is greater than the sum of the contributions

- UNCONDITIONAL LOVE—they are accepting without reservation

Anytime I interact with people and I see evidence of these signals, I know I'm connecting. I've learned what it takes to connect with others, and I've learned to gauge when I'm succeeding.

How are you doing when it comes to connecting? When you interact one on one with someone important in your life, do you receive these signals? When you lead a meeting or attend a group function, are these connecting characteristics evident? When you speak to an audience, do you connect with them in such a way that you're not only effective at communicating, but it's also a highly enjoyable experience for you and them? If you can't answer these questions with a resounding yes, then you need to improve your ability to connect with people. Everyone talks. Everyone communicates. But few connect. Those who do connect take their relationships, their work, and their lives to another level.

If you want to learn how to connect and thereby become more effective in everything you do, there's good news. Even if connecting with others isn't something you're good at today, you can learn how to do it and become better tomorrow. And that's why I wrote this book. I have learned how to connect well with people, and it is one of my greatest strengths. It's one of the main reasons I am able to communicate with people. It is a foundational part of my leadership. And I'm even learning how to connect with people using new technology. In fact, I put this manuscript on my blog, JohnMaxwellonLeadership.com, so that I could connect with people on this subject and get their input and feedback. The chapters received more than 100,000 views during the eleven weeks they were posted. More than seventy quotes, stories, and anecdotes from readers made it into the book, and I made nearly one hundred changes and improvements to the manuscript based on people's comments. I even asked the people who commented to submit photographs to be included in the book. The images on the cover and in the endpapers of this book are of the people who took the time to give their input and make the book better.

But that wasn't my primary motivation for posting the manuscript, nor is that my motivation for being on Twitter or using other new technology. I do these things because I want to add value to people. In 1979, I began writing books to make an impact on people I would never have the opportunity to meet in person. In 2009, I began blogging and using social media to expand my circle of connection with people even further. Now I can also add value to people who may never read one of my books. It's just another way to connect with people.

I am convinced that I can help you to learn how to connect with other people. That's the reason I wrote *Everyone Communicates, Few Connect*. In the first part of the book, I'll teach you the five principles that are foundational for understanding how to connect with people. In the second part, you'll learn five practices that anyone can do to connect with others—regardless of age, experience, or natural ability. Learning to connect with people can change your life.

Ready? Let's get started.

PART I

CONNECTING PRINCIPLES

1

CONNECTING INCREASES YOUR INFLUENCE IN EVERY SITUATION

According to experts, we are bombarded with thirty-five thousand messages a day.[1] Everywhere we go, everywhere we look, someone is trying to get our attention. Every politician, advertiser, journalist, family member, and acquaintance has something to say to us. Every day we are faced with e-mails, text messages, billboards, television, movies, radio, Twitter, Facebook, and blogs. Add to these newspapers, magazines, and books. Our world is cluttered with words. How do we choose which messages to tune in and which ones to tune out?

At the same time, we also have messages we want to get across to others. I've read that, on average, most people speak about sixteen thousand words a day.[2] If you transcribed those words, they'd fill a three-hundred-page book every week. At the end of a year, you would have an entire bookcase full of words. In a lifetime, you'd fill a library. But how many of your words would matter? How many would make a difference? How many would get through to others?

Talk is easy. Everybody talks. The question is, how can you make your words count?

How can you *really* communicate with others?

CONNECTING CAN MAKE YOU OR BREAK YOU

People cannot succeed in life without communicating effectively. It's not enough just to work hard. It's not enough to do a great job. To be successful, you need to learn how to really communicate with others.

> *It's not enough just to work hard. It's not enough to do a great job. To be successful, you need to learn how to really communicate with others.*

Have you ever gotten frustrated while making a presentation because people just weren't getting it? Have you ever wanted your boss to understand how much value you add to the company so you could get a well-earned raise or promotion? If you have children, have you wanted them to listen so you could help them make good choices? Have you wanted to improve your relationship with a friend or make a positive impact on your community? If you can't find a way to communicate effectively, you won't be able to reach your potential, you won't succeed in the way you desire, and you'll be forever frustrated.

What's the secret? Connecting! After more than forty years of marriage, a long and successful career as a public speaker, decades of leading various organizations, and experience in helping people develop across the United States and in dozens of countries around the world, I can tell you this: if you want to succeed, you must learn how to connect with others.

CONNECTING IS KEY

I am convinced more than ever that good communication and leadership are all about connecting. If you can connect with others at every level—one-on-one, in groups, and with an audience—your relationships are stronger, your sense of community improves, your ability to create teamwork increases, your influence increases, and your productivity skyrockets.

What do I mean when I say "connect"? Connecting is the ability to identify with people and relate to them in a way that increases your influence with them. Why is that important? Because the ability to communicate and connect with others is a major determining factor in reaching your potential. To be successful, you must work with others. And to do that at your absolute best, you must learn to connect.

> *Connecting is the ability to identify with people and relate to them in a way that increases your influence with them.*

How much healthier would your relationships be if you excelled at connecting? How would your marriage and family life improve? How much happier would your relationships with friends be? How much better would you be at getting along with your neighbors if you were able to connect with them?

How would being a better connector impact your career? What would happen if you were fantastic at connecting with your coworkers?

How would things change at work if you were better able to connect with your boss? According to the *Harvard Business Review*, "The number one criteria for advancement and promotion for professionals is an ability to communicate effectively."[3] That means connecting! If you learned to connect better, it would change your life!

CONNECTING IS CRUCIAL FOR LEADERS

I am probably best known for my writing and speaking on leading. If you want to become more productive and influential, learn to become a better leader because everything rises and falls on leadership. And the best leaders are always excellent connectors.

> *"The number one criteria for advancement and promotion for professionals is an ability to communicate effectively."*
>
> —HARVARD BUSINESS REVIEW

If you're interested in a case study in connecting in the context of leadership, all you have to do is look at the presidents of the United States from the last thirty years. Because every move of those presidents is documented in the press at home and around the world, most people are familiar with them.

Presidential historian Robert Dallek says that successful presidents exhibit five qualities that enable them to achieve things that others don't: vision, pragmatism, consensus building, charisma, and trustworthiness. As leadership and communication consultant John Baldoni points out,

Four of these factors depend heavily upon the ability to communicate on multiple levels. Presidents, like all leaders, need to be able to describe where they are going (vision), persuade people to come along with them (consensus), connect on a personal level (charisma), and demonstrate credibility, i.e., do what they say they will do (trust). Even pragmatism depends on communications . . . So in a very real sense, leadership effectiveness, both for presidents and for anyone else in a position of authority, depends to a high degree upon good communication skills.[4]

And what do those communication skills depend on? Connecting!

Set aside your political opinions and biases for a moment and look at the abilities of some past presidents. Consider the differences in connecting skill between Ronald Reagan and Jimmy Carter when they ran against one another. In their final debate on October 28, 1980, Carter came across as cold and impersonal. To every question he was asked, Carter responded with facts and figures. Walter Cronkite described Carter as humorless. Dan Rather called Carter stoic and disengaged. And as Carter made a case to be reelected, he seemed to bounce back and forth between trying to impress people by stating cold facts and trying to make his listeners feel sympathy for him and the burden of his job. At one point he stated, "I alone have had to determine the interest of my country and the involvement of my country," and he stated, "It's a lonely job." He never focused on his audience and their concerns.

In contrast, Reagan was engaged with his audience and even with Carter. Before the debate, Reagan walked over to Carter to shake his hand, which seemed to startle the president. During the debate, when his opponent spoke, Reagan listened and smiled. When it was Reagan's turn to speak, his appeals were often directed to his audience. He wasn't trying to come across as an expert, though he did quote figures and dispute some of Carter's facts. He was trying to connect. Many remember his closing remarks, in which he asked people, "Are you better off than you were four years ago?" Reagan told his audience, "You made this country great." His focus was on the people. There couldn't have been a greater contrast between the Great Communicator and his predecessor.

A similar contrast can be seen between Bill Clinton and his successor, George W. Bush. Clinton took communication to the next level as president. He equaled Reagan's ability to connect one-on-one as well as on camera. When he said, "I feel your pain," most people around the country connected with him. Clinton not only possessed Reagan's connection skills but also added to them a mastery of the interview and talk show formats, which was critical when he ran for election. He seemed never to miss an opportunity to try to connect. So far, no politician has surpassed him in connecting with others.

Bush, on the other hand, seemed to miss nearly *every* opportunity to connect with people. His one clear moment of connection occurred immediately after September 11, 2001, when he spoke at Ground Zero. After that he usually fumbled and flopped when he tried to speak with others. His inability to connect alienated people and colored everything he did as president.

Communication expert Bert Decker publishes a list every year of the top ten best and worst communicators of the year. Guess who was on the worst communicator list every year during his last term in office? That's right, President George W. Bush. In 2008, Decker wrote about Bush, "Soon after [9/11] he slipped back to the shrugs and smirks, and tangles of syntax and grammar. It perhaps reached a nadir in the response to Katrina. Such is not the communications

of a leader. Having so little influence this past year, it is sad to put our president as the #1 worst communicator of 2008."[5]

If you follow politics, you probably have a strong opinion about Jimmy Carter, Ronald Regan, Bill Clinton, and George W. Bush. You can say what you will—either positive or negative—about their character, philosophy, or policies. But their effectiveness as leaders was definitely impacted by their ability or inability to connect.

Connecting is crucial whether you're trying to lead a child or a nation. President Gerald Ford once remarked, "If I went back to college again, I'd con-

> *"If I went back to college again, I'd concentrate on two areas: learning to write and to speak before an audience. Nothing in life is more important than the ability to communicate effectively."*
>
> —GERALD FORD

centrate on two areas: learning to write and to speak before an audience. Nothing in life is more important than the ability to communicate effectively." Talent isn't enough. Experience isn't enough. To lead others, you must be able to communicate well, and connecting is key.

CONNECTING HELPS IN EVERY AREA OF LIFE

Of course, connecting isn't just for leaders. It's for anyone who desires to be more effective at what he or she does or enjoy better relationships. I received many comments from people on my blog, JohnMaxwellOnLeadership.com, affirming this.

I heard from business people such as Tom Martin, who described the importance of connection in his work. "To connect is to join, but to make a connection there has to be rapport," wrote Tom. "This is what I try to help our sales force to see as their role in transitioning a lead into a prospect, a prospect into a customer, and a customer into a client. It is those connected clients who become our greatest advocates to help us grow our business."[6]

I also heard from many teachers and trainers. Exceed Resources trainer and coach Cassandra Washington told me, "In the classroom, I teach that connection is key. Leadership is about connecting with people. Serving customers is about connecting. Raising kids . . . connecting."[7] An English as a Second Language teacher, Lindsay Fawcett, wrote that when she was in Hong Kong and mainland China, she noticed that whenever she went to a meeting, there was always a connection time planned before it started, with food and drinks provided so that people could get to know one another. It changed her perspective. "I am one of those people who grew up being able to do 'things' well, but I never understood the idea of connecting. I finally learned to connect with my students, which has helped me become a better teacher."[8]

Jennifer Williams, who had just moved into a new neighborhood, said that she went out of her way to meet new neighbors, talk to them, discover their occupations, and learn the names of their children and pets. As she did, people began to come together. "Wow," one neighbor told her, "until you moved in, we rarely talked, didn't know each other, and would never sit out in the evenings and socialize. Here you've been for less than two months, and you know everyone!" Jennifer says it's because "people want to be made to feel connected and a part of something."[9] I agree, but I also recognize that she is a connector!

When people possess the ability to connect, it makes a huge difference in what they can accomplish. You don't have to be a president or high-profile executive for connecting to add value to you.

Connecting is vital for any person who wants to achieve success. It is essential for anyone who wants to build great relationships. You will only be able to reach your potential—regardless of your profession or chosen path—when you learn to connect with other people. Otherwise, you'll be like a nuclear power plant disconnected from the grid. You'll have incredible resources and potential, but you will never be able to put them to use.

THE DESIRE TO CONNECT

I am convinced that nearly anyone can learn to connect with others. Why? Because I learned how to do it. Connecting wasn't something I did naturally. When I was a kid, I wanted to connect with my parents, not just because I loved them but also because I suspected that if I had a good connection with my mother, it might keep me from getting a spanking when I misbehaved.

I also learned that humor could be very valuable for connecting. I remember one time when my older brother, Larry, and I got into trouble and laughter saved me. Usually when we were punished, we were asked to bend over and grab a chair. Then Mom would give us a couple of whacks on the seat of our pants with a pancake spatula. Larry, as the oldest, usually went first, and on this occasion, when Mom gave him the first whack, there was a loud *bang*, and a puff of smoke emerged from Larry's hind end. The explanation? Larry had a roll of caps stored in his back pocket. Mom just howled. We all ended up laughing, and best of all, I didn't get a spanking that day! For three weeks, I kept caps in my back pockets—just in case.

As I got a little older and entered school, I became aware that some kids connected with the teachers while I didn't. In first grade,

Diana Crabtree was the student who connected. In second grade, it was Elaine Mosley, and in third grade, Jeff Ankrom. I could see that the teachers loved those kids. I wanted my teachers to like me too, and I started to wonder what my classmates were doing that I wasn't.

In junior high school, it was the same thing. When I tried out for the basketball team, I made the squad, but I didn't get to start, even though I was a better player than two of the other players who were starters. I could sense an invisible barrier that was keeping me from where I wanted to go. I felt frustrated. I wondered why Coach Neff liked them more than he liked me. What I discovered was that those students had connected with Coach during the previous year, and I hadn't. My lack of connection held me back.

Have you ever experienced similar things? Maybe you are the most skilled person in an area at work, yet you never get promoted. Or you work hard and produce, but others don't seem to appreciate what you do. Or maybe you desire to build relationships with people around you, but they don't seem to listen to you the way they do to others. Or you want to create an effective team—or just become part of a good team—but you are made to feel like an outsider. What's the problem? It's connection. To succeed with other people, you need to be able to connect.

I finally started to learn about connecting in high school. My wife, Margaret, and I started dating then. She was very popular, and there were three other young men besides me who were interested in her. To be honest, she had her doubts about me. I was always trying to impress her, but she was suspicious whenever I lavished compliments on her. "Hmph," she'd say. "How can you say that? You don't even know me that well!"

How did I stay in the game? I decided to connect with her mother! Once I won over Margaret's mother, I gained some time to win over

Margaret. And whenever I did something stupid, which I must admit was too often, Margaret's mother would defend me. It helped me to win Margaret's confidence and, years later, her hand in marriage.

> *When you connect with others, you position yourself to make the most of your skills and talents.*

My awareness of the importance of connecting with people was acute by the time I went to college. I knew that it could make the difference between success and failure. People whom I saw connect with others had better relationships, experienced less conflict, and got more things done than those who didn't connect. Have you ever heard of someone who is said to live a "charmed life"? Usually those are people who have learned how to connect. When you connect with others, you position yourself to make the most of your skills and talents. When you don't connect, you have a lot to overcome just to get to average, a neutral starting position.

I was working from a deficit position. I had a lot of ambition and clear goals during college and the early years of my professional life, but my inability to connect with people was a barrier to my success.

THE COURAGE TO CHANGE

Are you familiar with the Serenity Prayer made famous by theologian Reinhold Niebuhr and adopted by many twelve-step programs? It says,

God grant us the serenity to accept the things we cannot change,
courage to change the things we can, and
wisdom to know the difference.

That prayer describes how I felt as I came face-to-face with my inadequacy in connecting with other people. I felt like I was suspended between my inadequacy and my desire to change. What I needed was to "know the difference" between what I could and couldn't improve. Simply recognizing that I was coming up short wasn't enough. If I couldn't change and improve in this vital area of my life, it meant success would be forever out of reach. I wanted to be able to connect with people all the time, not just occasionally on a hit-and-miss basis.

During that season I took stock of my communication skills, and here is what I figured out.

THERE WERE THINGS I COULD CHANGE BUT DIDN'T KNOW HOW TO CHANGE

I could see that I wasn't connecting with others, but I didn't know why I was coming up short or how to make up the difference. I wished someone in my circle of relationships could help me, but the people I could ask for help weren't connecting with others either. The one good thing about this season is that it got me started thinking about how to solve the problem.

MY COPING SKILLS WERE GREATER THAN MY CONNECTING SKILLS

What do you do when you're frustrated or you fail? Most people either crash, cope, or change. Fortunately, my upbringing had been good; I had a positive self-image and attitude. So I was able to cope. Unfortunately, coping isn't moving forward. It's static and inherently defensive in nature. It's reactive. Merely coping doesn't help anyone accomplish anything. It merely keeps a person afloat. What I wanted was change.

To communicate effectively and to lead others, you have to take initiative. You have to be proactive. You need to do more than merely cope. I recognized that. If I wanted to be a person who moved forward, led others, and ran a successful organization, I needed to move beyond coping. I needed to be connecting.

I WANTED TO MAKE A DIFFERENCE, NOT JUST KNOW ABOUT THE DIFFERENCE

There are times in life when you realize there are things you cannot do. In those moments, you decide either to accept it or to fight for it. I decided to fight. Why? Because I wanted to make a difference in the lives of others, and I knew that if I didn't learn how to connect with other people, my ability would be forever limited. I wasn't willing to just live with my shortcomings. I wanted to do something about them.

I NEEDED MORE THAN COURAGE TO CHANGE THINGS—I NEEDED CONNECTING SKILLS

Honestly, the Serenity Prayer feels a bit passive to a naturally proactive leader like me. I wanted more than just the courage to know and accept the difference between what I could and could not change. I wanted the courage and energy and skills to make the changes needed to go the distance. I wanted to become a connector able to have a positive influence on the lives of others. I wanted to learn to connect with anyone at any time.

MORE TALK ISN'T THE ANSWER

No matter what your goals are, connecting can help you. And if you can't connect, it will cost you. Of course, there are also other benefits of learning to connect with people and communicate with them effectively, as illustrated by a humorous story a friend sent me about Jorge Rodriguez, an Old West bank robber from Mexico who operated along the Texas border around 1900. Rodriguez was so successful that the Texas Rangers established a special force to try to stop him.

> No matter what your goals are, connecting can help you.

Late one afternoon, one of these Rangers saw Rodriguez slipping across the border back into Mexico and trailed him at a discreet distance. He watched as the outlaw returned to his home village and mingled with the people in the square. When Rodriquez went into his favorite cantina to relax, the Ranger slipped in and managed to get the drop on him.

With a pistol to the bank robber's head, the lawman said, "Jorge Rodriguez, I know who you are. I've come to get back all the money that you have stolen from the banks in Texas. Unless you give it to me, I am going to blow your brains out."

Rodriguez could see the man's badge and could discern his hostile intent. But there was a problem. He didn't speak English. He began speaking rapidly in Spanish. But the Ranger couldn't understand what he said, because he didn't speak Spanish.

Just then a young boy came up and said in English, "I can help. I speak English and Spanish. Do you want me to be your translator?"

The Ranger nodded. The boy quickly explained everything the Ranger had said.

Nervously, Rodriguez answered, "Tell the big Texas Ranger that I have not spent a cent of the money. If he will go to the town well, face north, and count down five stones, he will find a loose one there. Pull it out, and all the money is behind there. Please tell him quickly."

The boy looked back at the Ranger and said, "Señor, Jorge Rodriguez is a brave man. He says he is ready to die."

Okay, so the story is probably more humorous than true, but it makes a point. Connecting with others may not be a matter of life or death for most of us, but it often is a matter of success or failure. I think the further along in life we get, the more aware we become of the importance of connecting with others. It's the basis for the social networking movement on the Internet. People are eager to connect with others, and most will do anything they can to feel connected.

It Starts with Your Attitude

The ability to connect with others begins with understanding the value of people. Jim Collins, author of *Good to Great*, observes, "Those who build great companies understand that the ultimate throttle on growth for any great company is not markets, or technology, or competition, or products. It is the one thing above all others—the ability to get and keep enough of the right people." You do that by connecting with these people.

> *The ability to connect with others begins with understanding the value of people.*

Herb Kelleher, former chairman and CEO of Southwest Airlines, did that. I was reminded of this on May 21, 2008, when I saw an ad in *USA Today* from the Southwest Airlines Pilots' Association. It had a picture of a napkin with airline routes written on it, and the text of the ad said:

Thank You, Herb!

From cocktail napkin to cockpit, Herb Kelleher paved the way for the most spirited Company in airline history.

As you step down from the SWA Board of Directors, the pilots of Southwest Airlines would like to thank you, Herb, for 38 years of positively outrageous service to our Company and our pilots. It has been an honor and a privilege.

Herb Kelleher did what all of the most effective people do. He connected. He let people know he cared about them, not just at Southwest Airlines, but evidently wherever he went. Newspaper and magazine publisher Al Getler attended a conference in San Francisco where Kelleher was scheduled as the luncheon speaker. Al and some friends sat at a table in the empty ballroom an hour early when Kelleher walked in.

"Herb," Al shouted, "come over and join us!" To his surprise, Kelleher did. He joked with them, learned their names, and chatted with them about their experiences on his airline. When Al told Herb his sister had just flown Southwest for the first time, Kelleher joked that he should tell her never to fly on any other airline.

"You tell her," Al shot back. When he dialed his sister's number on his cell phone, Kelleher cheerfully took the phone and left the message on her voice mail. The whole group howled.

"Herb Kelleher could have continued to walk by us to do his sound check and then enjoy a meal before his speech," commented Al. "Instead he stopped, took the time and connected with every single person in that group."[10]

Jay Hall of the consulting firm Teleometrics has studied the performance of sixteen thousand executives and found a direct correlation between achievement and the ability to care for and connect with people. Here are a few of his findings:[11]

HIGH ACHIEVERS	AVERAGE ACHIEVERS	LOW ACHIEVERS
Care About People as Well as Profits	Concentrate on Production	Are Preoccupied with Their Own Security
View Subordinates Optimistically	Focus More on Their Own Status	Show a Basic Distrust of Subordinates
Seek Advice from Those Under Them	Are Reluctant to Seek Advice from Those Under Them	Don't Seek Advice
Listen Well to Everyone	Listen Only to Superiors	Avoid Communication and Rely on Policy Manuals

Clearly, if you want to have an advantage in working with people, you need to learn to connect!

TO BE EFFECTIVE IN ANY AREA OF LIFE, CONNECT

If you already work at connecting with people, you can learn to become even better at it. And if you haven't previously tried to connect with others, you will be astounded by how it can change your life.

Cathy Welch, who sings as a member of a trio, wrote to tell me of a visit she made to a nursing home. She said,

In the runaround business of finding someone in the facility who could give us permission to move dining tables in order to set up our equipment, I stood at the closest nurses' station and quietly waited for someone to ask. While I waited, I noticed a lady in a wheel chair with her back to me, her head hunched over almost in her lap. She sat motionless, her right arm on the counter of the nurses' station. She seemed completely drawn in to herself.

Since we were there to encourage and minister to the seniors in this home, I felt drawn to go around this woman, lean down and ask her how she was. Expecting no response, it took my breath away when she turned her head toward me, lifted her head a few inches and with delight on her face she said, "I'm fine! My name is Abigail and I used to be a school teacher."

I could only imagine how long she had waited for someone to notice her. People are people everywhere and in every situation, wouldn't you say?[12]

Yes, people are people. And wherever you find them, they desire to connect with others!

If you are facing connecting challenges, as I was early in my life and career, you can overcome them with connecting choices. You can become more effective by learning to connect with every kind of person in any kind of situation.

I can help you. Because I have learned to connect with others and because I have helped many others to learn how to connect, I feel certain I can also help you. My desire is first to help you learn the principles behind connecting with others, by:

- Focusing on others

- Expanding your connecting vocabulary beyond just words

- Marshalling your energy for connecting
- Gaining insight in how great connectors connect.

Then I'll help you acquire the practical skills of connection:

- Finding common ground
- Making your communication simple
- Capturing people's interest
- Inspiring them, and
- Being authentic.

These are things anyone can learn to do.

I believe that almost everything we become and all that we accomplish in life are the result of our interaction with others. If you also believe that to be true, then you know that the ability to connect with others is one of the most important skills a person can learn. It's something you can begin to improve starting today. This book will help you do it.

CONNECTING WITH PEOPLE AT ALL LEVELS

Throughout this book, the focus is on connecting with others at three different levels: one-on-one, in a group, and with an audience. At the end of each chapter, there will be questions or assignments to help you apply the ideas in the chapter to your own life in these three areas.

CONNECTING PRINCIPLE: Connecting increases your influence in every situation.

KEY CONCEPT: The smaller the group, the more important it is to connect.

CONNECTING ONE-ON-ONE

Connecting with people one-on-one is more important than being able to do it in a group or with an audience. Why? Because 80 to 90 percent of all connecting occurs on this level, and this is where you connect with the people who are most important to you.

How good are you at connecting with friends, family, colleagues, and coworkers? To increase your influence one-on-one:

- Talk more about the other person and less about yourself. Prepare two or three questions you can ask someone before a meeting or social gathering.

- Bring something of value, such as a helpful quote, story, book, or CD, to give to someone when you get together.

- At the close of a conversation, ask if there is anything you can do to help them and then follow through. Acts of servanthood have a resounding impact that live longer than words.

CONNECTING IN A GROUP

To connect with a group, you must take initiative with the people in the group. To do that, do the following:

- Look for ways to compliment people in the group for their ideas and actions.

- Look for ways to add value to people in the group and what they're doing.

- Don't take credit when the group succeeds, and don't cast blame when it fails.

- Find ways to help the group celebrate successes together.

CONNECTING WITH AN AUDIENCE

One of the best ways to learn how to connect with an audience is to observe communicators who are good at it. Learn from them and adopt what you can into your own style. Meanwhile, here are four things you can do to connect with an audience:

- Let your listeners know that you are excited to be with them.

- Communicate that you desire to add value to them.

- Let them know how they or their organization add value to you.

Tell them that your time with them is your highest priority that day.

2

CONNECTING IS ALL ABOUT OTHERS

Have you ever been excited about sharing an experience with someone important, only to have it unexpectedly ruined? That's what happened to me several years ago.

While I was on a business trip to South America, I got the chance to visit Machu Picchu, the mountaintop home of the ancient Inca, considered one of the Seven Wonders of the World. My guide was fantastic, the view was amazing, and the whole experience was incredible. When I returned home, I was determined to take my wife, Margaret, there.

Not long afterward, we picked a date and invited our close friends Terry and Shirley Stauber to go with us. To make the visit even more special, we made reservations to stay at a sixteenth-century monastery converted into a fine hotel in Cusco. And we booked tickets on the luxury train run by Orient Express. I wanted to make this once-in-a-lifetime experience as special as possible.

GREAT EXPECTATIONS

With great anticipation we boarded the train with the Staubers and our friends Robert and Karyn Barriger, who have lived in Peru for twenty-five years. They had been to Machu Picchu many times, but they agreed to join us as our unofficial hosts and guides. As the train made the long climb through the countryside, we were not disappointed. The gorgeous scenery that glided along outside our windows for three and half hours made us feel as though we were in a *National Geographic* special. The food and service on the train were spectacular, and the conversation with our friends was warm and engaging.

We arrived at the station at noon and took a bus up to the ancient city. We climbed aboard along with six other people and Carlos, our tour guide. As we rode to the top of the mountain, I tried to connect with Carlos. I've found that we usually have a better experience if I get to know our guide and he or she gets to know us. I tried making conversation with Carlos, asking questions about his background and his family in an attempt to get to know him, but he never really engaged. His answers were pleasant but short. I liked him, but I quickly realized that he wasn't really interested in me or anyone else in the group. And he wasn't going to do anything to connect with us.

Machu Picchu is truly one of the most beautiful places on earth. The lush green landscape against a crystal-blue sky makes it feel as if you can reach out and touch the nearby mountain peaks. The view of the river flowing in a massive gorge at the edge of the ancient city is breathtaking.

As soon as we got off the bus, the deep sense of history in the place was overwhelming. We tried to soak it in, but Carlos quickly gathered us around and started his prepared speech. It seemed that what he wanted to say to us was much more important to him than any of us were. For the next four hours, we found ourselves in information overload. Carlos bombarded us with facts and figures, dates and details. The spectacular experience I'd had on my previous visit and that I had hoped to share with Margaret and my friends was ruined by Carlos and his barrage of boredom-inducing information. Any question we asked was an inconvenience to Carlos. When someone wanted to take a picture in order to record a cherished memory, Carlos quickly brought us back to his lecture. It was clear that Carlos didn't place any value on us, his listeners.

With each passing minute, a greater sense of disinterest settled into our group. In time, we began to feel that we were an interruption to Carlos and his agenda. Before long, I observed that the members of the group were drifting away one by one. They were separating themselves from Carlos both physically and emotionally.

By mid-afternoon, the group had scattered, and Carlos was talking to thin air. From a distance I watched in amazement as Carlos lectured to no one but himself, continuing the tour without his group. Only as time ran out and the bus was preparing to leave did people go anywhere near him.

NOT GETTING THE MESSAGE

A good guide draws others in. After reading my story about Carlos, floral designer Isabelle Alpert wrote that while on a tour in Hawaii, her enthusiastic and caring guide embraced the group and made everyone feel part of the island. "I will treasure that tour forever, for it became a part of me," commented Isabelle. "Even though my initial expectation was just to see the scenery, unbeknownst to me, I really wanted to be *in* the scenery."[1]

24

Carlos made the same mistake as others who don't connect: they see themselves as the center of the conversation. Many people have commented to me how they fell into this in their businesses. Barb Giglio told about an experience she had when she sold Revlon products. "I talked so much and so fast about what I was selling," she says, "I assumed my customers were mother and daughter, and it turned out they were sisters! I insulted the two of them and humiliated myself."[2] Gail McKenzie, a fitness trainer and life coach, remarked, "I often have to help a client decide what's next. I have not had the success that I selfishly thought I would have in growing my business, and I think I see why. I haven't been really connecting. I have been the tour guide with an agenda. WOW and OUCH."[3]

This kind of self-centeredness happens in every aspect of life and on every level of business. Joel Dobbs told me the story of a new CEO who failed to lead the company through a crisis because he never did anything to connect with the people in his organization. Instead, he isolated himself from his employees and stayed in his huge office in the executive suite. Joel says,

> On the rare occasion when his schedule called for him to attend a meeting in another building, instead of walking across the beautiful campus the few hundred yards to the other building (where he might, God forbid, encounter an actual employee) he would travel down his private elevator to the private garage where his driver would drive him to the other building. There he would be met by security guards who would usher him to the elevator, which was empty and waiting, and then take him to the floor where his meeting was to be held . . . His isolation and lack of connection with the company's employees made it impossible for him to lead through

the crisis, and as a result the board replaced him. The new CEO was, and still is, a great communicator and connector. One of his first actions was to reconfigure the executive suite. He told a group of us that in addition to the former CEO's office being "obscenely large," the windows faced away from the corporate campus! The new CEO took a smaller office with windows that faced his people. He connected with the company's employees and led a successful turnaround.[4]

This, of course, isn't a phenomenon only in business. I've known many teachers and speakers who possess that self-focused mind-set. Every conversation is about them. Every communication is an opportunity for them to demonstrate their brilliance and share their expertise. My friend Elmer Towns, a professor and dean at Liberty University, once told me that self-centered teachers seem to share a common philosophy:

> Ram it in—jam it in,
> Students' heads are hollow.
> Cram it in—slam it in,
> There is more to follow.

Such people miss incredible opportunities in life by failing to connect. Good teachers, leaders, and speakers don't see themselves as experts with passive audiences they need to impress. Nor do they view their interests as most important. Instead, they see themselves as guides and focus on helping others learn. Because they value others, they work at connecting with the people they are teaching or trying to help. Music teacher Pete Krostag says, "I connect with my students in order for them to connect with an audience. I have also noticed as a musician that whenever I connect with the music and not with my own ego, the audience shares in the experience. A musical experience can be lost when the musician focuses on himself and not on the music because the audience loses out on the experience of sharing the moment."[5]

I admit that when I began my career as a minister, I didn't understand this. I was detrimentally self-focused. When I counseled people who were experiencing difficulties, my attitude was, *Hurry up and finish telling me your problem so I can give you my solution.* When I was leading any kind of initiative, I constantly asked myself, "How can I get people to buy into my vision so that they'll help me with my dreams?" When I spoke to an audience, I was focused on myself and not them. I lived for positive feedback, and my goal was always to be impressive. I even wore glasses to make me look more intellectual. When I think about it now, I shudder in embarrassment.

Much of what I did was all about me, yet I still wasn't succeeding. I was often self-centered, and that was at the root of most of my problems and failures. I was too much like the guy in this cartoon by Randy Glasbergen:

"There is no *I* in *TEAM*. But there is an *M* and an *E* and that spells *ME!*"

I felt frustrated and unfulfilled. I kept asking myself questions like, "Why aren't people listening to me? Why aren't people helping me? Why aren't people following me?" Notice my questions centered on me because my *focus* was on me. When I made a call to action, it often began with my interest above everyone else's. Me, me, me! I was self-absorbed, and as a result, I failed to connect with people.

THE LIGHTBULB MOMENT

Then something happened that changed my attitude. When I was twenty-nine years old, my dad invited my brother-in-law, Steve Throckmorton, and me to attend a Success Seminar in Dayton, Ohio. Growing up, I had heard some great preachers. Some spoke with fiery passion. Others were masters of rhetoric. But at this seminar, I heard a speaker who understood how to connect with people. I sat there mesmerized.

At the time, I remember thinking, *This is someone who understands success. I like him. But there's more to it than that—he really understands me. He knows what I believe. He understands what I'm thinking. He knows what I feel. He can help me. I would love to be his friend. I already feel like he's my friend.*

That speaker was Zig Ziglar. His way of connecting with an audience totally changed my thinking about communication. He told stories. He made me laugh. He made me cry. He made me believe in myself. And he shared insights and tips I could take away from the event and apply personally. That day, I also heard him say something that changed my life: "If you will first help people get what they want, they will help you get what you want." Finally, I understood what had been missing from my own communication—and from my interaction with other people. I saw how selfish and self-centered I'd been. I realized that I was trying to get ahead by correcting others when I should have been trying to connect with others.

> *I was trying to get ahead by correcting others when I should have been trying to connect with others.*

I walked away from that seminar with two resolutions. First, I would study good communicators, which is something I have done ever since. Second, I would try to connect with others by focusing on them and their needs instead of my own.

IT'S NOT ABOUT ME!

Connecting is never about me. It's about the person with whom I'm communicating. Similarly, when you are trying to connect with people, it's not about you—it's about them. If you want to connect with others, you have to get over yourself. You have to change the focus from inward to outward, off of yourself and onto others. And the great thing is that you can do it. Anyone can. All it takes are the will to change your focus, the determination to follow through, and the acquisition of a handful of skills!

Why do so many people miss this? I think there are many reasons, but I can tell you why I missed it and why I thought communicating and working with others was all about me.

IMMATURITY

When I began leading and communicating with others professionally, I was young and immature. I was in my early twenties, and I did not see the big picture. I saw only myself; everyone and everything else was in the background. Donald Miller, the author of *Blue Like Jazz*, likens such immaturity to thinking that life is like a movie in which you are the star. That's the way it was for me. Too many of the goals I pursued and tasks I completed were about my desires, my progress, my success. I look back now and marvel at how selfish my attitude was.

Maturity is the ability to see and act on behalf of others. Immature people don't see things from someone else's point of view. They rarely concern themselves with what's best for others. In many ways, they act like small children.

Margaret and I have five grandchildren. We delight in spending time with them. But like all small children, they don't spend their time focused on what they can do for others. They never say, "Papa and Mimi, we want to spend the entire day taking care of you and entertaining you!" Nor do we expect that of them. We focus on them. We recognize that part of the parenting process is helping children understand that they are not the center of the universe.

> *Maturity is the ability to see and act on behalf of others.*

I love something I read recently called "Property Law as Viewed by a Toddler" by Michael V. Hernandez. If you have children or grandchildren—or if you've ever spent time with a toddler—you'll find that it rings true:

1. If I like it, it's mine.

2. If it's in my hand, it's mine.

3. If I can take it from you, it's mine.

4. If I had it a little while ago, it's mine.

5. If it's mine, it must never appear to be yours in any way.

6. If I'm doing or building something, all the pieces are mine.

7. If it looks like it's mine, it's mine.

8. If I saw it first, it's mine.

9. If I can see it, it's mine.

10. If I think it's mine, it's mine.

11. If I want it, it's mine.

12. If I need it, it's mine (yes, I know the difference between "want" and "need"!).

13. If I say it's mine, it's mine.

14. If you don't stop me from playing with it, it's mine.

15. If you tell me I can play with it, it's mine.

16. If it will upset me too much when you take it away from me, it's mine.

17. If I (think I) can play with it better than you can, it's mine.

18. If I play with it long enough, it's mine.

19. If you are playing with something and you put it down, it's mine.

20. If it's broken, it's yours (no wait, all the pieces are mine).[6]

As people grow older, we hope their self-centered attitude will soften and their mind-set will change. In short, we expect people to mature. But maturity does not always come with age; sometimes age comes alone.

> *Maturity does not always come with age; sometimes age comes alone.*

Deep down, most of us want to feel important. But we need to fight against our naturally selfish attitude, and believe me, that can be a lifelong battle. But it's an important one. Why? Because only mature people who are focused on others are capable of truly connecting with others.

EGO

There is a very real danger for people with public professions to develop unhealthily strong egos. Leaders, speakers, and teachers can develop a disproportionate sense of their own importance. My friend Calvin Miller, in his book *The Empowered Communicator*, uses the form of a letter to describe this problem and the negative impact it has on others. The letter says:

Dear Speaker:

Your ego has become a wall between yourself and me. You're not really concerned about me, are you? You're mostly concerned about whether or not this speech is really working . . . about whether or not you're doing a good job. You're really afraid that I will not applaud, aren't you? You're afraid that I won't laugh at your jokes or cry over your emotional anecdotes. You are so caught up in the issue of how I am going to receive your speech, you haven't thought much about me at all. I might have loved you, but you are so caught up in self-love that mine is really unnecessary. If I don't give you my attention it's because I feel so unnecessary here.

When I see you at the microphone, I see Narcissus at his

mirror . . . Is your tie straight? Is your hair straight? Is your deportment impeccable? Is your phraseology perfect?

You seem in control of everything but your audience. You see everything so well, but us. But this blindness to us, I'm afraid, has made us deaf to you. We must go now. Sorry. Call us sometime later. We'll come back to you . . . when you're real enough to see us . . . after your dreams have been shattered . . . after your heart has been broken . . . after your arrogance has reckoned with despair. Then there will be room for all of us in your world. Then you won't care if we applaud your brilliance. You'll be one of us.

Then you will tear down the ego wall and use those very stones to build a bridge of warm relationship. We'll meet you on that bridge. We'll hear you then. All speakers are joyously understood when they reach with understanding.
—Your Audience[7]

The first time I read Calvin Miller's letter, I was struck by how accurately it described me when I came out of college. I was so cocky. I thought I had everything figured out, but the truth is that I didn't have a clue. I had taken courses in speaking, but the university course work I had completed for my degree had merely taught me how to construct a competent outline. My studies in no way prepared me to connect with an audience. Our professors had encouraged us to concentrate our attention on our subject. We were told to focus our eyes at a point on the back wall of the room. My delivery was awkward and mechanical. Worse yet, whenever I spoke, I wasn't very interested in the people to whom I was speaking; I was looking for the compliments I hoped to receive after the message. Nobody can connect with that kind of attitude.

FAILURE TO VALUE EVERYONE

Today I see my purpose as adding value to others. It has become the focus of my life, and anyone who knows me understands how important it is to me. However, to *add value* to others, one must first *value* others. In the early years of my career, I didn't do that. I was so focused on my own agenda that I often overlooked and ignored many people. If they weren't important to my cause, they didn't get my time or attention.

> *To* add value *to others, one must first* value *others.*

I think this wrong attitude is very common. One of the best stories I've ever read that illustrates this point is told by a nurse. She explains:

> During my second year of nursing school our professor gave us a quiz. I breezed through the questions until I read the last one: "What is the first name of the woman who cleans the school?" Surely this was a joke. I had seen the cleaning woman several times, but how would I know her name? I handed in my paper, leaving the last question blank. Before the class ended, one student asked if the last question would count toward our grade. "Absolutely," the professor said. "In your careers, you will meet many people. All are significant. They deserve your attention and care, even if all you do is smile and say hello." I've never forgotten that lesson. I also learned her name was Dorothy.[8]

To succeed in life, we must learn to work with and through others. One person working alone cannot accomplish much. As John Craig points out, "No matter how much work you can do, no matter how engaging your personality may be, you will not advance far in business if you cannot work through others." That requires you to see the value that others possess.

When we learn to turn our focus from ourselves to others, the whole world opens up to us. This truth is understood by successful people in every walk of life in every part of the world. At an international meeting of company executives, one American businessperson asked an executive from Japan what he regarded as the most important language for world trade. The American thought the answer would be English. But the executive from Japan, who had a more holistic understanding of business, smiled and replied, "My customer's language."

If you are involved in any kind of business, having a good product or service isn't enough. Becoming an expert on your product or service isn't enough. Knowing your product but not your customers will mean having something to sell but no one to buy. And the value you place on others must be genuine. As Bridget Haymond commented, "You can talk till you are blue in the face, but people know in their gut if you really care about them."[9]

INSECURITY

The final reason people often place too much focus on themselves and not on others is insecurity. I admit, this was not one of my problems as I started my career. I grew up in a very positive and affirming environment, and I did not lack confidence. However, that isn't the case for many people.

Chew Keng Sheng, a lecturer at Universiti Sains Malaysia's School of Medical Sciences, believes that the underlying reason for immaturity and ego-centeredness, especially among public speakers, is insecurity. "I can remember the first few times when I was asked to speak," wrote Keng Sheng. "I was literally shaking. When the speaker is insecure, he will seek approval from his audience. And the more he wants to seek approval from them, the more engrossed he becomes in himself and how he can impress others. As a result, he is more likely to fail to meet the needs of the moment."[10] What a negative cycle that can create, especially if a person doesn't receive or recognize the desired approval.

A MATTER OF CONNECTION

A couple of years ago, I spoke at an international conference in Dubai hosted by a company founded by Nabi Saleh. Nabi is an expert when it comes to coffee and tea. He began his career in 1974 working with tea and coffee plantations in Papua New Guinea, helping them with marketing and manufacturing, and has been active in that industry ever since, particularly in Australia. In 1995, he visited a coffee shop chain in the United States called Gloria Jean's that was begun by Gloria Jean Kvetko in Chicago. Nabi and his business partner Peter Irvine had such a high opinion of it that they secured the rights to open shops in Australia. In 1996, they opened two Gloria Jean's locations in Sydney, but they struggled.

They looked to their customers for the answer, and soon they figured it out. "We based our stores on the U.S. model," says Nabi, "which was totally un-Australian. People loved the coffee, they loved the product, but they said, 'Where are the seats, where is the food?' It was a take away concept. We knew if we kept going like that we would not be in partnership too much longer. So we started to re-format."[11]

They spent nearly two years tweaking their shops, refining and polishing the stores until they connected with their customers.

That's when Nabi and Peter began franchising. In ten years' time, they opened more than 300 stores.[12] In 2005, they bought the international rights to Gloria Jean's Coffees and expanded beyond the borders of Australia and the United States.[13] Today Gloria Jean's has 470 stores in fifteen countries around the world.[14]

Despite his business success, Nabi keeps everything in perspective. When we were at the conference together, Nabi told me, "We aren't in the coffee business, serving people. We're in the people business, serving coffee."

Nabi gives this advice to people in the service industry: "You have to have a service heart. You have to be prepared to serve the needs of those people you come into contact with. At all times it is to look at what it is the customer wants. It's not what I want, or what Peter wants, it's the person paying the dollars who is keeping us all going."[15] In other words, you have to remember that it's all about others. That's what it takes to succeed.

> *"We aren't in the coffee business, serving people. We're in the people business, serving coffee."*
>
> —NABI SALEH

THREE QUESTIONS PEOPLE ARE ASKING ABOUT YOU

Understanding that your focus must be on others is often the greatest hurdle people face in connecting with others. It's a matter of having the right attitude. But that alone is not enough. You must be able to communicate that attitude of selflessness. How do you do that? I believe you do it by answering three questions that people always ask themselves when interacting with others, whether as a client, customer, guest, audience member, friend, colleague, or employee.

1. "Do You Care for Me?"

Think about the best experiences you've had with people in your life. Really stop for a moment, and try to recall three or four of those experiences. What do they all have in common? I bet that the person or people involved in them genuinely cared about you!

Mutual concern creates connection between people. Aren't there certain friends and family members you simply want to spend

> Mutual concern creates connection between people.

time with? That desire comes from your connection with them. What's wonderful is that you can broaden your ability to care about others beyond your personal social circle. If you can learn to care about others, you can connect with them. You can help them. And you can make both your life and their lives better. It doesn't matter what your profession is. Take a look at these quotes from successful people from a variety of backgrounds:

BUSINESS: "You can't make the other fellow feel important in your presence if you secretly feel that he is a nobody."

—LES GIBLIN, former National Salesman of the Year
and popular speaker

POLITICS: "If you would win a man to your cause, first convince him that you are his sincere friend."

—ABRAHAM LINCOLN,
sixteenth president of the United States

ENTERTAINMENT: "Some singers want the audience to love them. I love the audience."

—LUCIANO PAVAROTTI,
legendary Italian opera tenor

MINISTRY: "I get a speech over [with] because I love people and want to help them."

—NORMAN VINCENT PEALE,

pastor and author

Connecting with others by caring about them goes beyond profession—and even beyond species, according to animal trainer Laura Surovik. As assistant curator at SeaWorld in Orlando, Florida, Laura works with killer whales. She wrote to say,

> I have been a trainer for twenty-four years, and I have been "connecting" and teaching others how to connect with Shamu for many years. Shamu has been one of my greatest teachers too. When you look into a killer whale's eyes, you realize that it is not about you. It can't be. The connection is made when they know that you are there for them—it's all about building trust through a loving, caring relationship. You must be sincere and worthy of being followed to connect and build a relationship with the ocean's top predator.[16]

That's true with everyday human beings as well.

Most people have a strong desire to connect with others, but they also have difficulty connecting. They are often preoccupied with their own worries and needs. As Calvin Miller says, when most people listen to others speak, they are silently thinking,

> *I am loneliness waiting for a friend.*
> *I am weeping in want of laughter.*
> *I am a sigh in search of consolation.*
> *I am a wound in search of healing.*

If you want to unlock my attention, you have but to convince me you want to be my friend.[17]

Whenever you can help other people to understand that you genuinely care about them, you open the door to connection, communication, and interaction. You begin to create a relationship. And from that moment on, you have the potential to create something beneficial for both you and them, because good relationships usually lead to good things: ideas, growth, partnerships, and more. People live better when they care about one another.

2. "CAN YOU HELP ME?"

One evening Tom Arington and I were having dinner, and I asked him questions about his success in business. Tom is the founder and CEO of Prasco, an independent pharmaceutical company. He told me he owed his success to one question he has always asked in any and every situation: "Can I help you?" By helping others, he has also helped himself. "Whenever people have a heart to do better," said Tom, "I help them if I can. What I found is that as I lifted others to a higher level, they lifted me up also."

> *Nobody wants to be sold, but everyone wants to be helped.*

There's an old saying in sales: nobody wants to be sold, but everyone wants to be helped. Successful people who connect with others always keep in mind that others are always asking themselves, "Can this person help me?" One of the ways they answer that question is to focus on what benefits they can offer someone.

In his book *Presenting to Win,* Jerry Weissman points out that when people communicate, they focus too much on the features of their product or service instead of answering the question, "Can you help me?" The key, says Weissman, is to focus on benefits, not features. He wrote:

> A Feature is a fact or quality about you or your company, the products you sell, or the idea you're advocating. By contrast, a Benefit is how that fact or quality will help your audience. When you seek to persuade, it's never enough to present the Features of what you're selling; every Feature must always be translated into a Benefit. Whereas a Feature may be irrelevant to the needs or interests of your audience, a Benefit, by definition, is always relevant.[18]

In our current world, people are bombarded with information daily about the features of this product or that gadget. They tend to tune it out. If you want to get someone's attention, show you can help.

3. "CAN I TRUST YOU?"

Have you ever bought a car? If so, how was the experience? For many people it's terrible because they don't trust the person who is trying to sell them the car. Much of the industry seems to be designed to keep its customers off balance, skeptical, and suspicious.

"Trust is even more important than love."

—JEFFREY GITOMER

Trust is vital to any business. In fact, it's vital to life itself. Author and speaker Jeffrey Gitomer told me that trust is even more important than love!

If you have bought a car, when you stepped into that car showroom, whether you were aware of it or not, you looked at the salespeople and internally asked the three key questions from the chapter:

1. Do you care for me?

2. Can you help me?

3. Can I trust you?

Chances are that during a bad car-buying experience you were unable to answer yes to all three of those questions. You may not have even been able to answer yes to *one* of them! As a result, you didn't connect with the people involved.

Naturally, that isn't everyone's experience. In fact, Emran Bhojawala wrote telling me about his experience with Lloyd, a car salesman in the Washington, D.C., area who was so helpful, dependable, and trustworthy when Emran bought a car as a student that he bought a vehicle from him even after Emran moved to Minnesota. "When I wanted to buy a car," Emran explained, "I didn't have to worry about anything. I told him my budget and flew to Virginia to pick up a car I had never seen." Emran then drove twenty-three hours to get home. "He is THE legend when it comes to selling cars in the area near my school," wrote Emran. "He does not advertise, and all his business comes from previous customers and references. I think that's a perfect example of success in connecting with people."[19] Or as Mike Otis put it, "Business goes where it wants to, but it stays where it's appreciated."[20]

IF I WERE YOU . . .

Whenever people take action, they do so for their reasons, not yours or mine. That's why we have to get on their agenda and try to see things from their point of view. If we don't, we're just wasting their time and ours.

Several years ago I spent a few days in New York City visiting some of the nation's top book publishers with Sealy Yates, my agent, and several key members of my team. Our goal was to receive a new book contract. Prior to meeting with the publishers, we spent a great deal of time dis-

> *Whenever people take action, they do so for their reasons, not yours or mine.*

cussing what we thought would be important to the executives we'd be meeting. Sealy briefed us on what was going on in the industry and gave us insight on individual publishing houses. One of the members of my staff went over key points he thought were important from my company's point of view. And we all asked questions and sought answers. We wanted to be well prepared.

The night before we were to have our first meeting, I spent some time alone in my hotel room mentally preparing for the next day. The questions I kept asking myself were these: *If I were a publisher talking to an author, what would I want to know? If I were in their position, what would I ask John Maxwell?* I believed that if I could answer those questions, there would be a good chance that I would be able to connect with them and be offered a good contract.

I came up with a lot of ideas, but the question that I continually came back to was this: "How many more books do you want to write?" I believed that was the key, so for two hours I thought about my answer to that question. I wrote down the list of books I wanted to write over the next several years. As the list grew, so did my excitement and anticipation I had for the coming day. And when we met with the first publisher the next morning, sure enough, a few minutes into our conversation about a potential contract, an executive said, "John, you've already written thirty books. How many more do you want to write?"

With great enthusiasm I shared the ideas and titles of ten books I knew I wanted to write. I think some of the people in the room were a bit surprised that I had such a quick answer and was so passionate about the subject. Yet as I enthusiastically shared the titles, they got excited too. Everybody began taking notes and asking questions. And I could tell from their responses which ideas excited them the most. We had connected! And all I had done was spend some time trying to think from the publishers' perspective and explore what would be important to them.

You can connect with others if you're willing to get off your own agenda, to think about others, and to try to understand who they are and what they want. If you really want to help people, connecting becomes more natural and less mechanical. It goes from being something that you merely do to becoming part of who you really are. If you're willing to learn how to connect, you will be amazed at the doors that will open to you and the people you will be able to work with. All you have to do is keep reminding yourself that connecting is all about others.

CONNECTING WITH PEOPLE AT ALL LEVELS

CONNECTING PRINCIPLE: Connecting is all about others.

KEY CONCEPT: Connecting begins when the other person feels valued.

CONNECTING ONE-ON-ONE

How can you connect with people one-on-one? By making them feel valued. How do you do that?

- Know what they value by being a good listener when you are with them.

- Find out why they value those things by asking questions.

- Share your own values that are similar to theirs.

- Build your relationship on those common values.

In that way, value is added to both of you.

CONNECTING IN A GROUP

The key to making others feel valued in a group or on a team is to invite participation. The smartest person in the room is never as smart as all the people in the room. Input creates synergy, buy-in, and connection.

To connect with people in a group setting . . .

- Discover and identify the strength of each person.

- Acknowledge the value of each person's strength and potential contribution.

- Invite input and allow people to lead in their area of strength.

CONNECTING WITH AN AUDIENCE

One of the reasons speakers fail to connect is that they give the impression that they and their communication are more important than their audience. That kind of attitude can create a barrier between a speaker and an audience. Instead, show your audience members that they are important to you by doing the following:

- Express your appreciation for them and the occasion as soon as you can.

- Do something special for them if you can, such as preparing unique content for them and letting them know that you have done so.

- See everyone in the audience as a "10," expecting a great response from them.

- As you finish speaking, tell them how much you enjoyed them.

3

CONNECTING GOES BEYOND WORDS

People watch a reality show on television where two equally talented people sing the same song. One of them gives the audience goose bumps; the other one leaves everybody cold. Why is that?

Two professors at a university teach the same class at the same time using the same prescribed syllabus and required textbook. Students stand in line at registration to get into the first teacher's class, while the other's class starts below capacity and dwindles to just a few students. Why?

Two managers work together running a restaurant. All twenty employees work regularly for each of them. When the first manager needs extra help and asks people to work late, they do so willingly. When the other manager makes the same appeal the next week, all the employees make excuses for why they can't stay. What's the reason for the difference?

Two parents raise a child together in the same household, enforcing the same rules. One parent gets cheerful compliance, and the other gets resistance. Why?

Shouldn't the words of the song evoke the same response in both singers? Shouldn't the same course be equally appealing to students? Shouldn't both managers expect to be given the same consideration? Shouldn't parents in the same household inspire the same reaction?

Intuitively, you probably know that the answer is no. But why? Because people respond to others based not merely according to the words that are used but on the connection they experience with that person.

Your Actions Speak So Loudly, I Can't Hear Your Words

When people try to communicate with others, many believe the message is all that matters. But the reality is that communication goes way beyond words. In an important study, UCLA psychology professor emeritus Albert Mehrabian discovered that face-to-face communication can be broken down into three components: words, tone of voice, and body language. What may come as a surprise is that in some situations, such as when verbal and nonverbal messages aren't consistent, what people see us do and the tone we use can *far* outweigh any words we say while trying to communicate. In situations where feelings and attitudes are being communicated:

- *What we say* accounts for only 7 percent of what is believed.

- The *way we say it* accounts for 38 percent.

- *What others see* accounts for 55 percent.[1]

Amazingly, more than 90 percent of the impression we often convey has nothing to do with what we actually say. So if you believe communication is all about words, you're totally missing the boat, and you will always have a hard time connecting with others.

While these statistics may reveal the limitations of words in some communication situations, they don't do anything to help us figure out *how* to better communicate with others. So what's the solution? Howard Hendricks, who has been a long-distance mentor to me for many years, says that all communication has three essential components: the intellectual, the emotional, and the volitional. In other words, when we try to communicate, we must include:

> *More than 90 percent of the impression we often convey has nothing to do with what we actually say.*

Thought: something we know
Emotion: something we feel
Action: something we do

I believe those three components are essential to connect with others as well. Fail to include any one of the three and there will be a disconnection from people and a breakdown in communication. More specifically, here's how I think the breakdown would occur. If I try to communicate:

- Something I *know* but do not *feel*, my communication is dispassionate.

- Something I *know* but do not *do*, my communication is theoretical.

- Something I *feel* but do not *know,* my communication is unfounded.

- Something I *feel* but do not *do,* my communication is hypo-critical.

- Something I *do* but do not *know,* my communication is presumptuous.

- Something I *do* but do not *feel,* my communication is mechanical.

When components are missing, the result for me as a communicator is exhaustion. However, when I include all three components—thought, emotion, and action—my communication has conviction, passion, and credibility. The result is connection. I believe you can achieve the same result when you include all three.

THE CHARACTERISTICS OF CONNECTION

Any message you try to convey must contain a piece of you. You can't just deliver words. You can't merely convey information. You need to be more than just a messenger. You must be the message you want to deliver. Otherwise, you won't have credibility and you won't connect.

> *Any message you try to convey must contain a piece of you.*

Have you ever had to communicate someone else's vision? It's very difficult to do, isn't it? It's hard to get excited when you're presenting someone else's ideas. Yet, if you work in any kind of organization and you're not the top leader, that is exactly what you are expected to do. How can you do that with credibility? By making it *your* vision. By that, I mean that you must first discover how the vision positively impacts you. You must connect with it on a personal level. Once you have done that, you will be able to do more than simply relay information. You will be able to convey inspiration. Nothing can happen through you until it happens to you.

> *Nothing can happen through you until it happens to you.*

This kind of ownership is necessary not only for leaders and speakers, but also for authors. For a book to connect with readers, it must be more than just a book. It must possess a part of the author. Otherwise it lacks authenticity and credibility. It can have great information, but it can still fall flat if the author does not connect with readers.

That's what I've always tried to do as an author: put part of myself into my books. I don't communicate anything that I haven't lived and learned from experience. I hope that comes through. For example:

- *Developing the Leader Within You* possesses conviction because I have developed myself to become a leader.

- In *Failing Forward*, I share proven ways I used to overcome my own failures.

- When I wrote *Winning with People*, I wanted the book to affect others the way Dale Carnegie's *How to Win Friends and Influence People* had impacted me as a teenager.

- *Thinking for a Change* shares the way that I think on a daily basis. My wife, Margaret, says it has more of my DNA than any of my other books.

51

- *The 21 Irrefutable Laws of Leadership* offers tried-and-true leadership principles I've used to equip more than four million people worldwide.

I work to make every one of my books more than just a book, more than just paper and ink or an electronic file to be offered in the marketplace. Every book comes from my heart and soul. I believe in it and genuinely hope it will help whoever reads it.

As important as it is for a message to be heartfelt and genuine, that of course isn't enough. Your message must also be more than just a message. It must have value. It must deliver on the promise it offers to its audience. It must have the potential to change other people's lives. That's my goal every time I write a book or prepare to speak to an audience.

Many times each year I am engaged as a speaker for companies and other organizations. Often I request a call with someone in the organization prior to the speaking engagement so I can learn the expectations of my host and the background of my audience. My goal is never to simply deliver a speech. I want to add value to people. And to have a chance to do that, what I say and do must be within the context of the bigger picture of the organization's purpose, mission, and goals. I always spend time tailoring what I'm going to say to fit what they need.

After I've finished speaking, I also take time to evaluate whether I connected with my audience and helped my sponsor. I do that by going through my Connection Checklist, which includes the following questions:

- INTEGRITY—Did I do my best?

- EXPECTATION—Did I please my sponsor?

- RELEVANCE—Did I understand and relate to the audience?

- VALUE—Did I add value to the people?

- APPLICATION—Did I give people a game plan?

- CHANGE—Did I make a difference?

If I can honestly answer yes to those questions, I feel certain that my connection with the audience was good and I was able to reward them for the time they've given me.

If you do any professional speaking, you may want to use a similar list to ensure that you are doing everything you can to connect. However, even if speaking isn't part of your work, there is still a principle that applies to you. When you take responsibility for connecting with others and you decide to serve others instead of yourself, your chances of connecting with people increase dramatically. Your attitude often speaks more loudly than your words.

THE FOUR COMPONENTS OF CONNECTION

If you want to succeed in connecting with others, you need to be sure your communication goes beyond words. How can you do that? By connecting on four levels: visually, intellectually, emotionally, and verbally.

1. WHAT PEOPLE SEE—CONNECTING VISUALLY

Sonya Hamlin in *How to Talk So People Listen* advises that between hearing and sight, sight is the more important and powerful sense when it comes to communication. She wrote, "As a species, we remember 85 to 90 percent of what we see but less than 15 percent of what we hear. That means that if you want me to learn and remember, you must also support your words by showing your ideas to me. . . . You now need to use the power of the visual to help sustain your audience's interest and bring it to new levels of understanding."[2] She backs this up with the following evidence indicating how people today are more visual than ever:

- 77 percent of all Americans get about 90 percent of their news from television.

- 47 percent get *all* their news from television.

- Major U.S. corporations have their own television studios.

- Video and Web conferencing are replacing on-site face-to-face sales meetings.

- Digital video recording systems are becoming commonplace in homes and offices.

- Children now log about twenty-two thousand hours watching television by age nineteen, more than twice the time spent in school.[3]

We live in a visual age. People spend countless hours looking at YouTube, Facebook, Vimeo, PowerPoint, video games, movies, and other media. You can certainly understand the importance of what can be seen in our culture. People expect any kind of communication to be a visual experience.

Anytime you are in front of other people to communicate—whether it's on a stage, in a boardroom, on a ball field, or across a coffee table—the visual impression you make will either help or hinder you. Television executive, communication consultant, and author Roger Ailes, who penned *You Are the Message*, wrote in *Success* magazine:

You've got just seven seconds to make the right first impression. As soon as you make your entrance, you broadcast verbal and nonverbal signals that determine how others see you. In business, those crucial first seven seconds can decide whether you will win that new account, or succeed in a tense negotiation.

Are you confident? Comfortable? Sincere? Glad to be there? In that first seven seconds, you shower your audience with subtle "cues." And whether people realize it or not, they respond immediately to your facial expressions, gestures, stance, and energy. They react to your voice—the tone and pitch. Audiences, whether one or one hundred, instinctively size up your motives and attitudes.

People can perceive a lot in seven seconds. They can decide that they do not want to hear anything a speaker has to say, or they can be struck by how much they are attracted to someone. As abolitionist and clergyman Henry Ward Beecher asserted, "There are persons so radiant, so genial, so kind, so pleasure-bearing, that you instinctively feel good in their presence that they do you good, whose coming into a room is like bringing a lamp there."

If you want to increase your ability to connect with people visually, then take to heart the following advice:

Eliminate Personal Distractions. It almost goes without saying, but the first place to start when connecting visually is to increase the chances that people are paying attention to the right things and not being distracted. If you're well groomed and wearing the right clothing for your situation, then that's a good start. Countless numbers of people have lost sales opportunities, ruined job interviews, or been turned down for dates because their appearance didn't match someone else's expectations.

It's also wise to eliminate any distracting personal habits or tics. Ask family and friends if you regularly display behaviors that capture their attention and take their focus off of what you communicate. And if you do any kind of public speaking, one of the best things you can do is capture yourself on video. John Love, a pastor who commented on my blog, wrote, "I never realized how many nonverbal mistakes I was making until I saw myself on video. Now it is my regular practice to go back and watch myself on tape to determine not only what I said, but also how I said it. The tape doesn't lie."[4]

Expand Your Range of Expression. Great actors can tell an entire story without uttering a word, simply by using facial expressions. And whether we are aware of it or not, we also convey messages with the expressions on our faces. Even people who take pride in wearing a poker face and who work hard not to crack a smile or let others know what they're thinking are conveying a message to others—detachment. And that makes connecting with others nearly impossible. If your face is going to "talk" for you anyway, you might as well have it communicate something positive.

> *If your face is going to "talk" for you anyway, you might as well have it communicate something positive.*

When my wife and I see our grandchildren, we go out of our way to *show* them how happy we are to see them. When they arrive at our house, we stop whatever we're doing to let them know how delighted we are to be with them, and we communicate that not only in words but also with smiles, hugs, and kisses. We want them to feel loved, accepted, and special every time we're with them.

When you are communicating to an audience, facial expressions become even more important. And in general, the bigger the audience, the more exaggerated the facial expressions need to be. Of course, technology has impacted the way people communicate with a large audience. I vividly recall my first experience speaking to an audience where I was filmed and my image appeared on a large video screen. It was at the Crystal Cathedral in Orange County, California. The large screen was several yards to my left, and I found it unnerving that people were looking over there instead of at me. But then I made a joke and made a facial expression to go with it that caused the audience to laugh, and I was relieved. Even though people were watching the screen instead of looking at me, I was connecting with them.

No matter who you are or with whom you are trying to communicate, you can improve your ability by smiling at people and being expressive. Even if you work in a tough environment or a staid corporate culture, you don't have to maintain a grim visage all the time. I figured this out early in life. When I was in the third grade, I remember looking at myself in the mirror one morning and thinking, *I am not a handsome guy. What am I going to do with a face like this?* Then I smiled. And I thought, *That helps.*

Move with a Sense of Purpose. When I was in college, I wanted to get a job at a local grocery store. So did my college friend Steve Benner, so he and I went together to apply for jobs. The manager met us at the front of the store and asked us to follow him to the back. There we filled out applications. Once we were done, he said he would let us know his decision about whom he would hire the next day. Steve got the job.

A few weeks later, I went to the manager to ask him why he didn't select me. I wondered if I'd put something on the application that worked against me. "It had nothing to do with the application," he responded. "I selected Steve because he walked to the back of the store briskly and with more energy than you did."

I have never forgotten that experience. Isn't it true that our perception of people differs based on how they carry themselves? One person garners attention while another gets ignored. One person commands respect while another doesn't. I've heard that robbers and pickpockets choose their victims based on body language. If somebody walks briskly, confidently, and alertly, criminals will often let them pass and look for another victim—someone lacking confidence and awareness.

Movement always conveys a clear message when someone desires to communicate. I am continually aware of this whenever I'm onstage. I move quickly and confidently onto the stage because I want people to know that I am eager to speak. I know that when I move closer to my audience, it helps to create a feeling of greater intimacy. And I try to keep from being too static. I know that if I move around every few minutes, people feel my energy and are more likely to stay engaged with me.

Maintain an Open Posture. Physical barriers are often some of the greatest hindrances to connection for someone trying to communicate. It took me years to figure this out and to become more effective in my communication. When I first started speaking to audiences, I usually stood behind a lectern and didn't move. As a result, I felt separated from my audience. When I began to walk around the stage and got out where people could see me, my connection with people improved greatly.

Becoming more physically connected to my audience helped me a lot. So did creating a psychological openness. I actually learned this by accident after I injured my back playing racquetball with my friend Patrick Eggers. The injury laid me up in bed for three days and threatened to prevent my going to a speaking engagement scheduled in Harrisburg, Pennsylvania. The only way I could fulfill my obligation was to bring my wife with me to help me get clothed and ready to speak, and to request that the host provide a stool for me to sit on.

I was able to keep my commitment, and during the process I made an astounding discovery. By using the stool, I had more energy than usual—even with an injured back. And I also felt more relaxed and connected with the audience. After analyzing the situation, I came to realize that while sitting, I was more conversational in my communication. That helped me to connect and made me much more effective.

Ever since then, I've been aware of the need to keep my physical and mental posture open to others when trying to communicate. When I'm in the office, I don't sit behind a desk when talking to someone. We sit in comfortable chairs facing one another with nothing between us. Or if we need to work, we sit side by side at a table.

Anytime you remove obstacles and reduce distance, connection becomes easier. And physical touch eliminates distance altogether. A handshake, a pat on the back, or a hug can do a lot to promote connection. Singer/songwriter Sue Duffield told me a story about her father that illustrates the power of touch and how it can help people connect:

I will never forget my dad's hands. He was a hardworking, blue-collar worker who abused his hands daily—yet somehow maintaining them to be immaculately manicured, tan and perfect . . . [One day] while I lay bruised and injured on a stretcher in an emergency room following a front-end collision, this seventeen year old was a complete wreck until I felt my dad's hand touch my shoulder. I knew immediately who it was without turning around. I felt his power, his sense of touch; a familiar calming and an instant connection that said, "It's OK".[5]

Do whatever you can to remove obstacles and close the gap between yourself and the person with whom you want to connect. And whenever it's appropriate, use touch to communicate that you care.

Pay Attention to Your Surroundings. Environment obviously plays an important role whenever we try to communicate with other people. Have you ever tried to connect with someone who's paying more attention to the television than to you? Have you tried to have a conversation in a loud area like a construction zone or during a concert? A difficult environment can make it hard or even impossible to connect.

If you desire to connect, you cannot afford to ignore your environment. That's true even if you have been asked to speak professionally. You can't assume that a setting is going to be conducive for connecting, even if it was supposedly designed for communication. That's why I always try to see the venue beforehand anytime I'm booked for a speaking engagement. I want to make sure nothing in the setup of the auditorium will hinder my time with the audience.

Steve Miller, my son-in-law, often works with me when I speak, and he usually arrives on-site before I do. He knows from experience what's needed for me to be able to connect with people. The first thing he checks is the proximity of the speaking area to the audience. That's very important to me. It can be hard to connect with an audience if it feels as if there is a gulf between me and them. I think this is true for many communicators. If you remember when Jay Leno became the host of *The Tonight Show*, you may recall the changes he made not long after he took over the show. When the host was Johnny Carson, he came out from behind a curtain to deliver his monologue. That suited him because his style was somewhat aloof. But that's not typical for most speakers. When Leno took over, he struggled the first few months. Why? Because the stage was not conducive to his communication style. However, as soon as the stage was redesigned, it worked for him. The curtain was removed, and a stage from which he could deliver his monologue was built very close to the audience. In fact, when Leno was hosting, whenever he was introduced, he shook hands with the front row of the audience before he started telling jokes. A change in environment made all the difference.

The second thing Steve looks at is the lighting. I want people to see me well onstage because I'm a visual communicator. But I also want good lighting for the audience for two reasons: I usually provide outlines and I want people to be able to take notes, and I want to be able to see the audience while I speak. Many of my connecting skills are responsive to others. When I see my audience well, I can sense what I need to do in order to enhance their response.

The third thing Steve checks is the sound system. Poor sound makes communication nearly impossible. I am continually amazed at the cheap sound systems that are provided in expensive hotels for conferences. Many have nothing better than a goose-neck microphone attached to a podium. Having to use that as a communicator is like an Olympic swimmer trying to win a race with his hands and feet shackled. Not only is the sound terrible, but it prevents the speaker from moving around or moving forward into the audience.

If you want to connect with others, you need to be willing to make adjustments. If you're trying to connect at home with your spouse, turn off the television. If you're planning to have lunch with a colleague or client, pick someplace quiet enough for you to carry on a conversation. If you're in charge of a meeting or small group get-together, pick the right room and make sure the setup works for everyone to be able to connect. And if you're preparing to speak to an audience, check the venue to remove obstacles to connection. Once you're already onstage, it will probably be too late to make any changes. To connect effectively, take responsibility for giving others the best chance to connect with you visually.

2. WHAT PEOPLE UNDERSTAND— CONNECTING INTELLECTUALLY

To effectively connect with people on an intellectual level, you must know two things: your subject and yourself. The first is rather obvious. Everyone's heard another person expound on a subject about which he knows nothing. At best it's comical. At worst it's torturous. But most of the time, it simply comes across as inauthentic. As jazz musician Charlie Parker once observed, "If you don't live it, it won't come out of your horn."

> *"If you don't live it, it won't come out of your horn."*
>
> —CHARLIE PARKER, MUSICIAN

I read a story about the great actor Charles Laughton that illustrates the difference between a merely good speaker and one who really knows what he's talking about. It's said that Laughton was attending a Christmas party with a family in London. During the evening the host asked everyone attending to recite a favorite passage that best represented the spirit of Christmas. When it was Laughton's turn, he skillfully recited Psalm 23. Everyone applauded his performance, and the process continued.

The last to participate was an adored elderly aunt who had dozed off in a corner. Someone gently woke her, explained what was going on, and asked her to take part. She thought for a moment and then began in her shaky voice, "The Lord is my Shepherd, I shall not want . . ." When she finished, everyone was in tears.

When Laughton departed at the end of the evening, a member of the family thanked him for coming and remarked about the difference in the response by the family to the two recitations of the psalm. When asked his opinion on the difference, Laughton responded, "I know the psalm; she knows the Shepherd."

There's no substitute for personal experience when we want to connect with people's hearts. If you know something without having lived it, your audience experiences a credibility gap. If you've done something but don't know it well enough to explain it, the audience experiences frustration. You have to bring both together to connect consistently.

As important as it is to know your subject, it's equally vital that you know yourself. Effective communicators are comfortable in their own skin. They're confident because they know what they can and can't do, and they gravitate to their communication sweet spot when they speak to people.

As I mentioned, it took me a while to learn this. I didn't start out as an effective communicator. My first experiences in public speaking were in 1967 while I was in college. At that time, my strategy was to imitate other speakers I admired. What a disaster! When that didn't work, I tried to impress people with my subject knowledge. Nobody listened! It took me eight years to "find myself" as a speaker. And here's great news: when you find yourself, you find your audience.

> *When you find yourself, you find your audience.*

3. WHAT PEOPLE FEEL—CONNECTING EMOTIONALLY

John Kotter, an author and a friend, recently wrote a book titled *A Sense of Urgency*. In it he states, "For centuries we have heard the expression, 'Great leaders win over the hearts and minds of others.'" Note that he didn't say that great leaders win over the minds of others. Nor did he say they win over others' minds and hearts. The heart comes first. And if we desire to be good communicators, we need always to keep that in mind. If you want to win over another person, first win his heart, and the rest of him is likely to follow.

I've witnessed a lot of speakers and teachers who rely too heavily on their intellect to persuade others. In addition, many of them also overestimate people's natural receptivity to the message and their desire to change because of it. These speakers and teachers believe that all they need to do is lay out a logical line of reasoning and people will be won over. It just doesn't work that way.

Therapist and leadership expert Rabbi Edwin H. Friedman remarked,

> The colossal misunderstanding of our time is the assumption that insight will work with people who are unmotivated to change. Communication does not depend on syntax, or eloquence, or rhetoric, or articulation but on the emotional context in which the message is being heard. People can only hear you when they are moving toward you, and they are not likely to when your words are pursuing them. Even the choicest words lose their power when they are used to overpower. Attitudes are the real figures of speech.

Whatever is inside of you, whether positive or negative, will eventually come out when you are communicating to others. The proverb

"As a man thinks in his heart, so is he" really is true. That comes across and impacts the way others react to you. People may *hear* your words, but they *feel* your attitude. That will either enable you to connect with people and win them over, or it will alienate them and cause you to lose them. In fact, your attitude often overpowers the words you use when speaking to others. As Jules Rose of Sloans' Supermarkets points out, "The exact words that you use are far less important than the energy, intensity, and conviction with which you use them."

> *People may* hear *your words, but they* feel *your attitude.*

People who are able to connect with others on an emotional level often have what could be called presence or charisma. They stand out in a crowd. Other people are drawn to them. As someone observed, "People will not always remember what you said. They will not always remember what you did. But, they will always remember how you made them feel."[6]

Why do some people have this ability? My friend and colleague Dan Reiland helped me understand this. One day he asked, "John, do you know why some people have charisma and others don't?"

"Personality," was my immediate response. "Some have a way with people and others don't."

"I don't think so," Dan responded. "I don't believe charisma is a function of personality. It's a function of attitude." He then explained how people with charisma possess an outward focus instead of an inward one. They pay attention to other people, and they desire to add value to them.

I have come to realize that Dan is right. People with "presence" have an unselfish attitude that causes them to put others first. They possess a positive attitude that prompts them to look for and focus on what's right instead of what's wrong. And they possess an unshakable confidence.

My favorite story about confidence comes from an interview Larry King did with Ty Cobb, one of the greatest baseball players of all time. Cobb, who was then seventy, was asked, "What do you think you'd hit if you were playing these days?"

Cobb, who was a lifetime .367 hitter (still the record), said, "About .290, maybe .300."

"That's because of the travel, the night games, the artificial turf, and all the new pitches like the slider, right?" Larry asked.

"No," responded Cobb. "It's because I'm seventy."

Confidence like that—when invested in others—helps people to feel connected to the person giving it, and it makes them confident in themselves.

Here's the bottom line on charisma. You don't have to be gorgeous, a genius, or a masterful orator to possess presence and to connect with others. You just need to be positive, believe in yourself, and focus on others. Do that, and there's a good chance you will connect with others because you make it possible for others to feel what you feel, which is the essence of connecting on an emotional level. That's true whether connecting with an audience, a small group, or one-on-one.

Steven Hiscoe, an instructor at a provincial police academy in Canada, trains police officers in self-defense and the use of force in difficult situations. He says that he tries to teach police officers how to connect on an emotional level after they've been in a violent confrontation. Steven explains, "When officers have been involved in a violent confrontation, they must then explain their actions to people who were not there but are acting as armchair quarterbacks." He teaches officers, "Don't just give them the facts, but include your emotion and perceptions, make them feel what you felt."[7] That is your goal anytime you want to connect with people. Help them to feel what you feel.

4. WHAT PEOPLE HEAR—CONNECTING VERBALLY

I hope that I have convinced you that communication goes way beyond words and that to connect with people we must appeal to them visually, intellectually, and emotionally. However, that doesn't mean that we should ignore the power of words!

As a writer and speaker, my life has been filled with words. My favorite games are word games such as Boggle and Upwords. My favorite pastime is reading. I love quotations. I believe, as British Prime Minister Benjamin Disraeli said, "The wisdom of the wise and the experiences of the ages may be preserved by quotations."

Listen to a speech by Martin Luther King Jr. and you will be inspired by his words. Read a play by Shakespeare, the world's greatest playwright, and you will hear phrases that are still in common use today—four hundred years later—and by people who don't even know they're quoting Shakespeare. Words are the currency of ideas and have the power to change the world.

What we say and how we say things make quite an impact. People respond to the language we use. The words we choose to speak to our spouse or children can either build them up or tear them down. They can make or break a deal. They can turn a boring talk into a memorable moment.

When I speak to others one-to-one, I'm careful to choose words that are positive and convey the confidence I have in them, even in a difficult situation. When I speak to an audience, I strive to make what I say punchy and memorable. As Mark Twain observed, "The difference between the almost right word and the right word is really a large matter—it's the difference between the lightning bug and the lightning."

How someone says something also communicates a lot. Hershel Kreis, an emergency communications supervisor, explains, "One of the handicaps for those of us in the 9-1-1 profession is that we can only communicate with our callers in the verbal realm." However, not being able to see the people who call doesn't stop them from gathering information and communicating effectively. "We can hear the pace of speech, background noise, tone, etc., but we learn through experience how to hear more than just the words being spoken by the callers and make a connection with the caller in spite of not having all of the nonverbal clues at our disposal."[8]

People pick up more than they might think from the way others say things. That's why I give that a lot of attention when I speak. Tone, inflection, timing, volume, pacing—everything you do with your voice communicates something and has the potential to help you connect to or disconnect from others when you speak.

PUTTING IT ALL TOGETHER

The art of communicating beyond words requires the ability to bring all four of those factors together—using the right words with the right emotion while being intellectually convincing and making the right visual impression. And all this needs to be done with the right tone of voice, the right facial expressions, and positive body language.

I know this sounds complicated. And it is. But it's also intuitive. The best advice I can give is for you to learn how to be yourself. The best professional speakers know themselves and their strengths—often learned through trial and error—and they use them to their greatest advantage. So do the best stand-up comics, politicians, entertainers, and leaders. Each has his or her own style, but they all share the ability to connect visually, intellectually, emotionally, and verbally.

If you haven't yet discovered and developed your style, study other communicators. Experiment when talking to people. It's okay to "borrow" effective techniques you see others using. Just make them your own. Don't do what J. Jayson Pagan confessed he tried once earlier in his career after hearing a message on CD that he loved and believed everyone in the organization needed to hear. "I listened to that CD and typed that message out word for word," Jayson explained. "When the time came I delivered it just the way I had heard it. Needless to say, I looked like a big green and blue parrot squawking repeats of what had impacted me. It had very little effect." Jayson sums up, "People need your influence, but it will not come through 'lip syncing' those you admire."[9]

> *"What you are speaks so loudly that I can't hear what you say."*
>
> —RALPH WALDO EMERSON

Your message must be your own. So must your style. Work to discover that style and to develop your skills as a connector in every kind of situation. And as you learn these skills, just remember how much of what you communicate is visual and goes beyond words. And remember the words of Ralph Waldo Emerson, who said, "What you are speaks so loudly that I can't hear what you say."

CONNECTING WITH PEOPLE AT ALL LEVELS

CONNECTING PRINCIPLE: Connecting goes beyond words.

KEY CONCEPT: The more you do to go beyond words, the greater the chance you will connect with people.

CONNECTING ONE-ON-ONE

People often overlook the importance of the nonverbal aspects of communication when trying to connect with one other person. They don't go the extra mile to connect beyond words. You improve in this area if you:

- Connect visually by giving the other person your complete attention. The eyes are the windows of the soul; see the other person's heart and show your heart.

- Connect intellectually by asking questions, listening carefully, and also paying attention to what isn't being said.

- Connect emotionally through touch (being careful to honor boundaries and remain appropriate with members of the opposite sex).

CONNECTING IN A GROUP

Connecting with a group is an excellent way to learn how to think and communicate like a coach. It's an interactive environment where you can actually show people what to do, and then you can ask them to demonstrate while you give them feedback. In group environments:

- Connect visually by setting the example. People in the group will do what they see.

- Connect intellectually by investing in people's growth. Build on what they already understand so they can develop to a higher level.

- Connect emotionally by honoring the group's effort and rewarding its work.

CONNECTING WITH AN AUDIENCE

Speaking to an audience is the most difficult of the three settings when it comes to communicating beyond words. Why? Because almost all of our communication from a stage is in words! However, you can still make immediate improvements to your nonverbal communication by doing three things, especially at the beginning of a presentation:

- Connect visually by smiling. This lets people know you're happy to be communicating with them.

- Connect intellectually by pausing strategically to give the audience time to think about something you've said.

- Connect emotionally through facial expressions, laughter, and tears.

4

CONNECTING ALWAYS REQUIRES ENERGY

T hink about the best public communicators you know. Make a mental list of three or four of them. Now think of a few people who are best at communicating to a small group or team. Now think of a few people who connect well with others one-on-one.

Thinking through your mental lists, consider this: how many of them are low-energy people? I'd be willing to bet the answer is none. Even when people come across as fairly low-key, they usually possess reserves of energy that are not evident on the surface. Why do I say that? Because connecting with other people doesn't just happen on its own. If you want to connect with others, you must be intentional about it. And that *always* requires energy.

THEY GET OUT OF IT WHAT YOU PUT IN

One of the most challenging and rewarding connecting opportunities I ever faced occurred in 1996. I received a phone call from a small church in Hillham, Indiana, inviting me to speak at a twenty-fifth anniversary celebration commemorating the building of their church. I could tell that the person making the request was nervous as he asked whether I would be willing to speak at the church. He also wanted to know how much it would cost.

The request, though unexpected, was one that I was pleased to receive. You see, I began my career in 1969 as the senior pastor at that small church in rural southern Indiana. While I was there, the attendance grew from a few people to a few hundred, and in 1971 we built a new church facility to accommodate the growing congregation. My career as a minister over the next two and a half decades may have taken me to larger churches and allowed me to make an impact beyond anything I had dreamed of back then, but I have always had a heart for the people of that congregation in Hillham. They gave me my start in my career and loved me unconditionally when I was young, inexperienced, and prone to make dumb mistakes. I immediately told him that I would happily return for such a wonderful occasion. Not only that, but I would also bring my family with me, and we would gladly pay all our own costs.

After I got off the phone, Margaret said, "John, I'm a little concerned about this event. Twenty-five years is a long time. You're not the person you were back then. You and they are in different worlds now. They may not relate to you. How are you going to connect with them?"

I thought about what my wife said for several days. She was right; I had changed a lot in those years. And I was sure they had changed too. It was going to take a lot of energy to connect with them. I couldn't just show up and expect things to work out on their own. To connect with the people, I had to figure out how to move toward them emotionally and relationally.

I knew the twenty-fifth anniversary reunion needed to be a special day for them, not me. I wanted to celebrate them, not just be there to celebrate. Over the next few weeks I reflected on my early years with the people in Hillham and decided to take action to do everything I could to build a connection. I did that by:

SEARCHING FOR REMINDERS OF OUR TIME TOGETHER

I went through my files, and I found records of weddings, funerals, sermons, and special events during our time together. One picture I found stood out above everything else. It showed 301 people standing in front of the church on a record attendance day. When I brought it to Hillham, the people loved finding themselves in the picture.

WORKING TO REMEMBER THEIR NAMES

I'm pretty good at remembering names because I really work at it. Some of the people at Hillham I will never forget, and their names will always come quickly to my tongue. But it had been a long time since I had been there, so I jogged my memory by going through records and photographs. By the time of the reunion, I remembered almost everyone's name. Better yet, when I arrived in the town, one of the members gave me a new pictorial church directory. It featured recent pictures of all the church's members, so I was able to see what everyone looked like now. I wish you could have seen their faces when I arrived at the church and was able to call people by name.

TRYING TO MAKE THEM FEEL SPECIAL

As part of the weekend celebration, I scheduled a gathering on Saturday with all of the members who had been in the congregation during my tenure. I didn't want anyone else to attend—just them. We spent three hours in the church basement revisiting the past. We looked together at memorabilia that made us laugh and sometimes brought us to tears.

MAKING MY VISIT PERSONAL FOR AS MANY PEOPLE AS POSSIBLE

I gave people copies of items such as baptism certificates and memorabilia from special moments. For example, I gave Shirley Crowder a copy of the sermon I preached the day she joined the church, and I gave Abe Legenour a picture of him being baptized. Everyone received something as a reminder of the "good ol' days." Then we took pictures of my family with every person.

GOING OUT OF MY WAY TO SPEND EXTRA TIME WITH PEOPLE

Some speakers and guest preachers arrive late, keep themselves separated from their audience, speak from the platform, and then leave as quickly as they can. I didn't want to do that. I wanted to make myself available to people. So Margaret and I went to the Sunday service thirty minutes early so we could personally greet as many people as possible. Much to my surprise, when we arrived, the parking lot was already full and the auditorium was jammed! I walked into the building and, row by row, greeted each person. After the service, we stayed around and were the last ones to leave.

SHARING MY MISTAKES DURING THE SERMON

I've learned that if you want people to be impressed, you can talk about your successes; but if you want people to identify with you, it's better to talk about your failures. That's what I did that day. And I thanked everyone for being so patient with me and so kind during those early years. Honestly, back then I was very green, and they put up with a lot. I was grateful and wanted them to know that.

ACKNOWLEDGING THEM AS PART OF MY SUCCESS

Nobody gets anywhere in life without the help of others. The people in that community helped me get on the right track in my career. I built my message on that fact and titled it "Ten Lessons I Learned at Hillham." As I spoke, they remembered, laughed, and cried. At the close of my message, I expressed sincere gratitude for their influence on my life. My last words to them were, "Every young pastor should spend their first years of ministry at Hillham. It would give them a foundation for a successful ministry."

I believe everyone enjoyed the reunion. Margaret and I certainly did. On the plane as we flew home, Margaret said, "Well, you did it. You connected with them." I felt satisfied that I had done my best. And I was worn out because it had taken a lot of energy.

YOU'VE GOT TO BRING IT

When I was working on my bachelor's degree, I took a speech class. More than forty years later, I can truly say that learning how to speak to an audience has been foundational to my journey through life as well as to my growth as a speaker. It was in that class that I heard what my professor called the "Four Unpardonable Sins of a Communicator": being unprepared, uncommitted, uninteresting, or uncomfortable. Do you notice the common denominator for three out of four of those "sins"? It's energy. The first three are a function of effort. It takes energy to be prepared, committed, and interesting! That is true whether you're speaking to one person or to one thousand. Connecting always requires energy.

Author and communication coach Susan RoAne, author of *How to Work a Room*, describes what it takes to connect with people in social settings. On her Web site she offers "Ten Tips from the

Mingling Maven," skills to be used when meeting new people. As you read her list, think about how many of them require energy. She says magnificent minglers:[1]

1. Possess the ability to make others feel comfortable

2. Appear to be confident and at ease

3. Have an ability to laugh at themselves (not at others)

4. Show interest in others; they maintain eye contact, self-disclose, ask questions, and actively listen

5. Extend themselves to others; they lean into a greeting with a firm handshake and a smile

6. Convey a sense of energy and enthusiasm—a joie de vivre

7. Are well rounded, well informed, and well-mannered

8. Prepare vignettes or stories of actual occurrences that are interesting, humorous, and appropriate

9. Introduce people to each other with an infectious enthusiasm (there is no other kind) that motivates conversation between the introducees

10. Convey respect and genuinely like people—the core of communicating

By my count, at least seven out of these ten require energy. If you want to connect with others but are hoping you can do so without being intentional, forget about it. Connecting always requires energy.

FIVE PROACTIVE WAYS TO USE ENERGY
FOR CONNECTING

It doesn't matter with whom or within what context you are trying to connect. It's always the same: you need to bring energy to do it effectively. And to make the most of connecting opportunities, you must channel that energy strategically. There are specific things you can do to help foster connection—with your spouse, at a social gathering, with coworkers or your boss, at a meeting, from a podium, or onstage in a stadium. I make that claim with confidence because I've connected with people in every one of those situations.

When I suggest that energy is required to connect with others, I'm not saying that you must be a high-energy person to connect with others. Nor do you have to be an extrovert. You must simply be willing to use whatever energy you have to focus on others and reach out to them. It's really a matter of choice. Engineer and project manager Laurinda Bellinger commented, "Twenty years ago, I had to make a decision to not hide behind my introverted personality and to connect with others. Now, when I tell people at work I'm an introvert, they laugh. But introverts can exhibit extroverted behavior—[however] it really drains us and we need to recharge sooner than an extrovert."[2]

If you want to connect with others, you need to be intentional about it. Here are five observations about the energy required to connect and what action you should take to be strategic in using that energy.

1. CONNECTING REQUIRES INITIATIVE . . . GO FIRST

I've had the privilege of speaking a few times to the employees of Wal-Mart at the company's headquarters in Bentonville, Arkansas. The first time I did so, I was taken on a tour of the facilities, where

I saw signs everywhere highlighting the values and philosophy of the organization. On that first visit after I had finished speaking, I took a notebook and jotted down the messages contained on many of the signs. The one that left the greatest impression on me was the "10 Foot Rule." It said,

> From this day forward, I solemnly promise and declare that every time a customer comes within ten feet of me, I will smile, look him in the eye, and greet him.
>
> —SAM WALTON

Sam Walton understood the importance of initiating contact with others. Initiative is to any relationship what a lighted match is to a candle.

I think most people recognize the value of initiative. They would readily admit that taking initiative is important in relationships, yet many still don't take it with others. When it comes to interacting with others, they often wait for the other person to take the first step. But all that does is lead to missed opportunities. Retired pastor Malcolm Bane observed, "If you wait until you can do everything for everybody, instead of something for somebody, you'll end up not doing anything for anybody." If you want to connect, don't wait. Initiate!

"If you wait until you can do everything for everybody, instead of something for somebody, you'll end up not doing anything for anybody."

—MALCOLM BANE

Willingness to expend energy to initiate connection is important not only with individuals but also with groups and teams. Simon Herbert, a coach at the Abbotsholme School in the UK, commented:

I'm in charge of my school's rugby programme, and last year I tried to remove myself from things a little more—a little less Coach and a little more from the players. I spent the rest of the season fire-fighting. I couldn't understand what was going wrong. Eventually, while on tour in South Africa, I pinned it down to the fact that I had stepped back from things a little, and my energy was no longer the driving force behind the teams. Don't get me wrong, I had some great leaders in the players and the coaches, but a close mentor let me know that it had clearly been my passion for the game and the players that had sparked the fire in all of the others, and I needed to keep adding the coal to keep the fire burning bright.[3]

Without Simon's willingness to go first and put his energy into the team, the team wasn't as successful as it otherwise could have been. Connection requires initiative.

One of the techniques I teach in *25 Ways to Win with People* is "Be the First to Help." It's very simple but also very powerful. Anytime in life that we find ourselves in need of assistance and we get some help, who is it that we remember most? It's usually the person who helps us first. Hasn't that been true for you? We are usually very grateful to the person who makes the effort to help or include us.

I know that's true for me. Les Stobbe was the first person to teach me about writing. Dick Peterson was the one who helped me start my first company. My brother Larry was the first to mentor me in business. Kurt Kampmeir initiated my journey in personal growth. Elmer Towns was the first to teach me about church growth. Gerald Brooks was the first to donate money to EQUIP, my nonprofit leadership organization. Linda Eggers saw that I needed help at my company and volunteered to assist me. It took energy and effort for them to do what they did for me, and each of these people will always have a special place in my heart! I have a connection with them that I have with few others.

A Jewish proverb says, "The wise does at once what the fool does at last." Too often, we wait for the "perfect moment" to initiate with others. It has been my experience that the perfect moment never arrives. Initiating a conversation with someone often feels awkward. Offering help to someone means risking rejection. Giving to others can lead to misunderstanding. You won't feel ready or comfortable in those moments. You just have to learn to get past those feelings of awkwardness or insecurity. As former first lady Eleanor Roosevelt said, "We must do that which we think we cannot." The people who connect with others are the ones who go ahead and do what the rest of us never quite got around to.

> *"The wise does at once what the fool does at last."*
>
> —JEWISH PROVERB

2. CONNECTING REQUIRES CLARITY . . . PREPARE

While connecting requires being willing to initiate with others, which often means taking action in the moment, it also requires that we know what we're doing when we make contact. That means having clarity of thought, and clarity most often comes as a result of preparation in three main areas:

Know Yourself—Personal Preparation. More than three decades ago when I was challenged to put myself on a personal growth program, I saw learning as a way to help myself. It wasn't long before I discovered that helping myself made me more capable of helping others. That's one of the reasons I tell people that to add value to others, they must make themselves more valuable. You can't give something you don't have. You can't tell what you don't know. You can't share what you don't feel. No one gives out of a vacuum.

Knowing yourself and growing yourself help you gain mental and emotional clarity. You know what you do and don't know. You know what you can and cannot do. You become comfortable in your own skin and confident in your identity. You are able to connect with others because you are willing and able to be open with people. What golf teacher and author Harvey Pinick says about professional golfers is true about people in other areas of life: "If a player was prepared for the little things, that player would be ready for the major challenges."

Know Your Audience—People Preparation. Connecting with people begins with knowing people. The more you understand about people in general, the better you will be able to connect. The more you know about the specific people you are trying to connect with, the better off you will be. If you don't have clarity concerning your listeners, your message will be muddy.

For years I have prepared and tailored my remarks to the people in the room. For example, when I lead roundtable meetings for leaders to discuss important issues in their field, I try to learn as much as possible about each of the people who attend. The more I know about them, the more clearly I can direct and help them. When I prepare for these meetings, I use a list similar to that of a journalist doing a story. I ask:

- Who are they?

- What do they care about?

- Where do they come from?

- When did they decide to attend?

- Why are they here?

- What do I have that I can offer them?

- How do they want to feel when we conclude?

Could I go into one of these roundtable meetings and just wing it? Probably. Would I be able to connect with people as well? No. Would I add value to them the way I would like? Absolutely not! It takes time and energy to answer these seven questions, but it's worth it. Anytime I want to connect with people, I expect to expend energy preparing beforehand.

Leaders constantly ask themselves questions like these as they bring people together in their organizations. They spend a great deal of time and energy asking questions, gathering information, preparing to meet with people. They know that if they want to cast vision, they have to bring clarity to the people in their organizations. The responsibility rests on their shoulders, not on those of the people listening to what the leaders have to say.

Know Your Stuff—Professional Preparation. Being yourself and understanding people will take you far in connecting with others. However, in situations where you must speak, teach, or lead, you must also be prepared professionally. You must know what you're talking about. I'm sure you've heard communicators who are great at connecting but have little to offer in terms of substance. After they speak, you walk away feeling good, but a few minutes, hours, or days later, you realize you're not better off than you were before.

Other times you come across people who have a lot to offer in terms of knowledge, but they cannot communicate effectively. Not long into their talk, you disengage. After they're done, you say, "Thank goodness that's over." Neither type of communication is effective. When someone can put it all together, the effect is powerful.

---

3. CONNECTING REQUIRES PATIENCE . . . SLOW DOWN

A young woman who was not accustomed to driving with a manual transmission stalled a car when a traffic light turned green. Each time she started the car, she nervously let the clutch out too fast and stalled it again. The car behind her could have gone around, but instead the driver laid on his horn. The more he honked, the more embarrassed and angry she became. After another desperate attempt to get the car going, she got out and walked back to the other car. The man rolled down his window in surprise.

"Tell you what," she said. "You go move my car, and I'll sit back here and honk the horn for you."

We live in an impatient culture. We use drive-through windows to buy meals, pick up our dry cleaning, complete banking transactions, and order prescriptions. I think Lisa Thorne's comment on my blog describes a lot of us: "The good news is I move fast; the bad news is I often move alone."[4] Everybody is in a hurry, but that prevents most of us from connecting with others effectively. If you want to connect with people, you need to slow down.

I must admit, impatience has always been a weakness for me, and I have continually had to work on it. Early in my career, I wanted to do things as quickly as possible and move on to the next thing. If someone didn't want to move at my speed, I breezed right past him or her. But that leadership style hindered my ability to connect with others, and my relationships suffered. The good news was that I moved fast. The bad news was that I often moved alone.

Moving at the speed of another person can be exhausting. It obviously takes energy to keep up with someone who is moving faster than we are. But isn't it also tiring to move at a slower pace than we want to? Henry David Thoreau wrote, "The man who goes alone can start the day. But he who travels with another must wait until the other is ready." I find waiting very frustrating. It tries my patience. However, if I want to connect with people, I have to be willing to slow down and go at someone else's pace. Good connectors don't always run the fastest, but they are able to take others with them. They exhibit patience. They set aside their own agendas to include others. These things require energy. But I've discovered over the years that anything really worthwhile in life takes time to build.

> *"The man who goes alone can start the day. But he who travels with another must wait until the other is ready."*
>
> —HENRY DAVID THOREAU

4. CONNECTING REQUIRES SELFLESSNESS . . . GIVE

In life, there are people who give and people who take. Which kind do you like to be around? Givers, of course. Everyone does. When we are in a grocery store or some other public place and see people we know to be takers, we tend to avoid eye contact or turn the corner quickly while pretending we haven't seen them. However, when we spot givers, we're glad to see them and we make it a point to greet them. It's easy to feel connected to givers.

Being a giver requires energy, and that's not always easy, especially in stressful situations. Motivational speaker Trudy Metzger, who overcame an abusive childhood, has become a giver in adulthood. However, she still finds it difficult to maintain a giver's mind-set when faced with some people from her difficult past. She sometimes becomes defensive and tries to control the situation if she feels vulnerable. Recently she realized that when that happens, she goes from being a giver to a taker. Says Trudy, "While giving requires energy, I have to say that the situations where I become a taker leave me completely drained and 'dead' inside. To be a giver brings life—like watering a plant so that it grows—but to be a taker is like sucking the water and nutrients from the soil, leaving both the plant and the soil depleted and useless."[5]

Being a giver can take a lot of energy. But so can avoiding interaction with others. Ed Higgins commented, "I consumed greater amounts of energy to avoid connecting (and I tend to be extroverted most of the time) and felt miserable by it. I came to realize that perhaps the energy used to not connect can be far greater than the energy it takes to connect."[6]

Being a giver is usually a win-win. It can energize you while it helps others. And it helps you to connect. That's true one-on-one, in a group, or with a large audience. If you focus on giving, you find it much easier to connect. In the years I was leading a church and preaching to the congregation most weekends, some of the staff and I would often spend time debriefing and discussing how the services had gone. During one of those sessions, my friend and colleague Dan Reiland said, "John, I think people find it really easy to listen to you."

"Can you explain what you mean?" I responded. I respect Dan and wanted to hear his perspective.

"I'll do even better than that," said Dan. The next morning, I had his written analysis on my desk. Here's what it said:

I thought about why you're so easy to listen to. The idea especially intrigued me when I thought about the fact that it's true even when people know the stuff you are going to say. And it definitely goes beyond the entertainment value of just good storytelling.

I think it all comes down to a communicator who is primarily a giver instead of a taker. The human spirit senses and feeds on a giving spirit. The spirit is actually renewed by a teacher with a giving spirit—this is proven by the fact that when people hear what you have said many times, they are still filled. Your teaching is essentially giving, and people can receive all day from a giver, while they tire quickly of a taker. Think about what Jesus taught—half the time the people didn't know what he was talking about, but they listened attentively. Jesus was giving—feeding them. Not taking. It was at a spirit (heart) level—he wasn't just giving information.

Here's how I think it works. If communicators teach out of need, insecurity, ego, or even responsibility, they are not giving. The needy person wants praise, something the audience must give. The insecure person wants approval and acceptance, something the audience must give. The egotistical person wants to be lifted up, to be superior and just a little bit better than everyone else, something the audience must give. Even the person motivated by responsibility wants to be recognized as the faithful worker, to be seen as responsible—something the audience must bestow upon them. Many communicators teach in one of these taking modes all the time and are not aware of it.

Then there's the giver. This person teaches out of love, grace, gratitude, compassion, passion, and the overflow. These are all giving modes. In each of these modes of the heart, the audience doesn't have to give anything—only receive. The teaching, then, becomes a gift. It fills and renews.

This is you. That's why people can listen all day. As I have watched and learned from you, you teach 99 percent of the time from the giving mode. Only very rarely do you slip into ego mode, and in those rare moments I no longer feel like you are giving. You are taking. That can come off as, "I am special and a little better than you." Other than those very rare moments, I could listen to you all day.

I don't think I'm as good a connector as Dan gives me credit for being, but I do always strive to focus on listeners and add value to them any way I can. However, I think he is exactly right about all speakers being either givers or takers, and it is definitely a function of attitude. Their mind-set is either selfless or selfish. We see others, as José Manuel Pujol Hernández suggested, as steps or bridges. If we see them as steps, we use them to raise ourselves up; if bridges, to connect.[7]

When you listen to someone speak, ask yourself, "Is the person giving me everything—eyes, face, body, brain, and personality? Or is this person simply passing through town and this opportunity to speak is just a stop along the way?" People who want to connect with others must give their all. And that takes energy!

Recently I was talking to a communicator who had grown bored from giving the same presentations again and again to different groups of people. I reminded him that he wasn't giving the presentation for himself; he was giving it for the benefit of others. How does one maintain that mind-set and find the energy to give everything he has every time he speaks?

In his book *Presenting to Win,* Jerry Weissman gives great advice on this. He says that speakers need to maintain "the illusion of the first time," a concept that comes from the world of stage actors. Though they may have to play a part dozens, hundreds, or even thousands of times, the audience needs to see a performance worthy of the first time. Weissman goes on to tell a story about Hall of Fame baseball player Joe DiMaggio:

A reporter once said to the Yankee Clipper, "Joe, you always seem to play ball with the same intensity. You run out every grounder and race after every fly ball, even in the dog days of August when the Yankees have a big lead in the pennant race and there's nothing on the line. How do you do it?"

> *Connection always begins with a commitment to someone else.*

DiMaggio replied, "I always remind myself that there might be someone in the stands who never saw me play before."

That is the kind of unselfish mind-set a person must maintain in order to connect with others. It takes a lot of energy, whether one-on-one, in a group, or in front of an audience, but it pays great dividends. Connection always begins with a commitment to someone else.

5. CONNECTING REQUIRES STAMINA . . . RECHARGE

Communicating with people can be very taxing physically, mentally, and emotionally. Author and consultant Anne Cooper Ready describes some of the emotions involved with speaking to an audience:

Public speaking is listed as Americans' number-one fear, before death at number five, and loneliness, weighing in at number seven. Guess that means that most of us are less afraid of dying alone than of making fools of ourselves in front of others. Fear is a powerful motivator for leadership, which means that you stand above the crowd. There is the fear of being seen as exceptional and different; the fear of the unknown; the fear of being a fraud; the fear of forgetting everything you were going to say; the fear of being at risk publicly; and the fear of being up there, alone. They all come together, for most of us, in public speaking.[8]

With all of this, how could working to connect with other people *not* drain a person of energy?

If we're not careful, connecting with people on a continual basis can so deplete us of energy that we have few reserves allowing us to do much of anything else. Even though I am an outgoing "people person," I still require a lot of private time to recharge my emotional, mental, physical, and spiritual batteries. I believe this is true for most speakers and leaders. Lorin Woolfe, in *The Bible on Leadership*, writes, "Leadership takes an almost bottomless supply of verbal energy: working the phones, staying focused on your message, repeating the same mantra until you can't stand the sound of your own voice—and then repeating it some more, because just when you start to become bored witless with the message, it's probably starting to seep into the organization."

Over the years I have learned how to keep my batteries charged. You'll need to do that, too, if you want to have energy available to connect with people. The first thing to do is to plug energy "leaks" by recognizing and avoiding what unnecessarily drains you of energy. Early in my career I spent a lot of time counseling people, and whenever I did I would come home exhausted. I remember wondering, *Why am I so tired?* After all, I was young and very excited about my career. It took me a while to figure out that sitting down with people to just listen to their problems left me devoid of energy.

Another energy drainer for me is working on the minute details of a project. It takes an inordinate amount of energy for a very limited return. As soon as I was able to hire people who are energized by detail work, I did. I'm a big believer in having myself and others work in their strength zones. Figure out what activities drain you of energy and avoid them if they're not essential.

You must also figure out what kinds of things fill your tank and leave you energized. Everybody's different. Johnson Tey wrote that he is energized by taking a stroll; Kasaandra Roache likes time at the beach. Ryan Schleisman spends time outside of the office with his staff. He says, "As a physician sometimes it's hard to get away to recharge. I know after I do, my patients and I are better because of it. My wonderful staff schedules recreation time for us. What an awesome plan."[9] I am recharged by a good massage, a round of golf, a change of pace, or prayer during my daily swim. And my favorite is spending a day with Margaret with no agenda. Pay attention to what charges your batteries and start making it part of your schedule.

> *"The only thing that keeps a man going is energy and what is energy but liking life?"*
>
> —LOUIS AUCHINCLOSS

If you are responsible for leading people or communicating with others, it is especially vital for you to find ways to recharge. It's really very simple. All you have to do is know the things you like to do and make time for them. As novelist Louis Auchincloss said, "The only thing that keeps a man going is energy and what is energy but liking life?" If you can carve out moments to do what energizes you, then you will always have reserves of energy you can draw upon when you want to connect with others.

To accomplish anything of value, you must learn to manage and marshal your energy. Performers and athletes understand this better than most people. If they don't do it, they don't get the results they desire. That was true for sportscaster Joe Theismann when he was a player in the NFL. He quarterbacked the Washington Redskins to two consecutive Super Bowl appearances in the 1980s. When his team played for the championship the first time in 1983, his attitude was positive and his energy was off the charts. He was excited to be there and gave everything he had. And his team won.

The next was totally different. He took a lot for granted, and his attitude wasn't good. Says Theismann, "I was griping about the weather, my shoes, practice times, everything." As a result, his performance suffered and the team lost. Was Theismann entirely responsible for the victory or the defeat? No, but as the quarterback, he was the team's leader, and he set the tone. I've been told he sometimes wears both his winner's ring and his loser's ring as a reminder of what he must do to be successful. "The difference in those two rings," says Theismann, "lies in applying oneself and not accepting anything but the best."

Connecting with others is like anything else in life: you have to be intentional about it. That doesn't mean you have to be loud or flashy. Business trainer Clancy Cross observed, "People often confuse energy with volume or speed. An accomplished musician knows that it requires more energy to sing or play slowly and softly (and connect with the audience) than it does to race and blast away. Even the way we sit with people and listen to them requires energy. They will detect when we do so without it. You can't fake energy and you can't fake a connection."[10]

To connect, you have to apply yourself and give your very best; otherwise you can't succeed at it. That takes energy—whether you're leading a meeting, having coffee with a friend, speaking to a large audience, or romancing your spouse. But I can't think of a better way to expend energy.

CONNECTING WITH PEOPLE AT ALL LEVELS

CONNECTING PRINCIPLE: Connecting always requires energy.

KEY CONCEPT: The larger the group, the more energy that's required to connect.

CONNECTING ONE-ON-ONE

Many people get lazy when it comes to connecting one-on-one. They take for granted that people will listen to them. But that's doing a disservice to others, especially the people who are closest to you, such as your friends and family.

Avoid that pitfall. The next time you try to connect with someone one-on-one, gear up for it mentally and emotionally, just as you would for an audience. If you bring intentional energy to the conversation, you make it much easier for people to connect with you.

If you're looking for ways to increase the energy one-on-one, then do what Margaret and I have done with each other for many years:

- Write on a piece of paper the significant things that happen to you during the day.

- For important things, tell no one else before sharing it with this specific person.

- Take time each day to go over your lists with each other, which requires intentionality and energy.

CONNECTING IN A GROUP

When you communicate with a group or in a meeting, the energy in the room can vary wildly. Sometimes the group will bring a lot of energy to the process and carry the day. Other times as the leader or communicator, you will need to marshal and generate energy.

The next time you communicate to a group, don't allow yourself to become complacent. Bring energy to the process and then continue bringing it—even if the energy in the room is good. Don't coast. The experience will be better for everyone if you remain intentionally energetic. In addition, you will gain people's respect if you take responsibility for the energy level.

A few times a year I lead a roundtable leadership session with fifteen to thirty executive-level leaders. Here are the guidelines I always follow with them:

- Before the session begins, I go to each person and introduce myself.

- I ask each individual a question to discover something unique about him or her.

- At the beginning of the session I give them ownership of the meeting. They ask me questions, and I do my best to serve them.

- If some are hesitant to enter in the discussion, I draw them in by telling the others about their uniqueness and how it relates to the subject.

- I end our time together by asking people how I can help them be more successful.

CONNECTING WITH AN AUDIENCE

No audience arrives at an event expecting to provide energy to the speaker. People come to shows, conferences, workshops, and events expecting to receive, not give. If you are the speaker, you must always keep that in mind. The larger the crowd is, the more energy you must provide.

Think about ways you can increase your energy when speaking to an audience. For example, confidence, which comes from preparation, brings energy. Passion, which comes from conviction, brings energy. Positivity, which comes from believing in people, brings energy. The more energy you bring to the process, and the better you are at conveying energy to your audience, the better your chances of connecting with them.

5

CONNECTING IS MORE SKILL THAN NATURAL TALENT

I'm going to do something unusual later in this chapter. I'm going to hand over the reins to Charlie Wetzel, my writer since 1994, so he can tell you some things about communication from his point of view. Charlie is a keen observer, a reflective thinker, and a longtime student of leadership and communication. He also knows me as well as any of my colleagues and has seen me in just about every kind of communication situation. I think you'll find his unfiltered perspective interesting, and he'll explain how we approach connecting in written form. But first, I want to tell you some things about people I consider to be great communicators.

COMMUNICATING ON THE HIGHEST LEVEL

Connecting is something anyone can learn to do, but one must study communication to improve at it. I've been a student of communication for four decades. Whenever I hear people speak, I not only listen to what they have to say, but I also pay attention to their style and technique as communicators. I occasionally attend events that feature communicators because I enjoy listening to them and learning from them.

Several years ago I went to a conference in San Jose, California, that featured ten well-known personalities. It was a diverse and interesting lineup of public figures, and I looked forward to seeing and hearing each one of them. I wanted to see which of them would connect with the audience and communicate effectively.

As I got ready to listen, I made a place in my notes for two columns and labeled them "Connector" and "Non-Connector." At the end of the day, I had written six names in the connector column and four in the other. I won't tell you the names of the non-connectors. (I feel certain you would recognize all of them.) However, I will describe their communication styles:

Non-Connector #1: This politician spoke entirely in a monotone. He droned on and on, his voice totally devoid of passion or conviction. He spoke almost as though we weren't even there. And we weren't even sure if *he* was there!

Non-Connector #2: Another politician, this speaker was pleasant enough. He conveyed a kind of grandfatherly persona. He spoke for about fifty minutes and said absolutely nothing.

Non-Connector #3: A Washington journalist, she spoke down to the audience. It was clear that she felt superior to all of us. I know she made me feel small. Everything she said sent one clear message: *I know something that you don't.*

Non-Connector #4: This speaker was a business book author, and to be honest, I was most looking forward to hearing him speak. However, I was surprised and disappointed by his angry demeanor.

His body language, facial expressions, and language displayed a negative attitude. I wouldn't have wanted to spend five minutes with him one-on-one. And he offered no practical application whatsoever during the time he spoke.

Each of these four speakers lost the audience. Some did it almost immediately. Others took longer. But in each case, you could tell the audience was relieved that the speaker's time was done. But when one of the good speakers—the six connectors—got onstage, you could feel the hope rise in the room. Here are the people who connected with the audience that day:

Mark Russell: A different kind of Washington insider, he has performed a comedy routine in the District of Columbia for more than twenty years. Mark had us laughing, but he also had us thinking. I bet he must have asked nearly a hundred questions during his session. Everyone was totally engaged.

Mario Cuomo: By far the most passionate speaker was the former governor of New York. He was electric. I could *feel* what he felt. He moved everyone in the room, and when he was finished, the entire audience stood and cheered.

C. Everett Koop: I have to admit that the nation's former surgeon general surprised me by how good a communicator he was. He was a master at using illustrations. He would make a logical statement, and then he would back it up and flesh it out with a great story. It was as if he were verbally putting a thumbtack in each note. After he spoke, I could recite all seven of his points from memory.

Elizabeth Dole: The former U.S. senator and president of the Red Cross made every person in the audience feel like her best friend. She possessed an easy confidence that made us glad to be there.

Steve Forbes: Of all the communicators I saw that day, I learned the most from him. The editor-in-chief of *Forbes* magazine was brilliant and informative. He made everything he talked about sound new.

Colin Powell: When the former U.S. Army general and Secretary of State spoke, he put everyone in the room at ease and gave us a sense of security. His voice and demeanor were confident, and when he spoke, he made us confident in ourselves. Most important, he gave us hope.

The excellent speakers in this lineup could not have been more different from one another. They had different backgrounds. They employed different speaking styles. They possessed different values. They spoke on different subjects. And they all had different talents and skill sets. They really had only one thing in common. They were excellent connectors. That's something that all great communicators and all great leaders have in common. And connecting is a skill that can be learned!

It's No Accident

Great communicators are not all cut from the same cloth. But they do all share the ability to connect. That does not develop by accident. You cannot expect to succeed through dumb luck, as did the leader of a wagon train of pioneers that was heading across the Western plains. When a lookout spotted a cloud of dust in the distance moving toward them, they knew they were in trouble. Sure enough, a tribe of Native American braves thundered toward them, and the leader ordered the wagons to form a circle behind a hill.

When the leader of the settlers saw the tall figure of a chief silhouetted against the sky, he decided to face the chief and attempt to communicate with him using sign language. Soon the chief backed away and returned to his men.

"What happened?" the pioneers asked the leader.

"Well, as you probably saw, we couldn't speak each other's language," he said, "so we used sign language. I drew a circle in the dust with my finger to show that we're all one in this land. He looked at the circle and drew a line through it. He meant, of course, that there are two nations—ours and his. But I pointed my finger to the sky to indicate that we are all one under God. Then he reached into a pouch and took out an onion, which he gave to me. Naturally, I understood that it indicated the multiple layers of understanding available to everyone. To show him that I understood his meaning, I ate the onion. Then I reached into my coat and offered him an egg to show our goodwill, but as he was too proud to accept my gift, he just turned and walked away."

Meanwhile the warriors were readying for an attack and awaited the order from their chief, but the old warrior held up his hand and recounted his experience.

"When we came face-to-face," he said, "we immediately knew that we did not speak the same tongue. That man then drew a circle in the dust. I know he meant that we were surrounded. I drew a line through his circle to show him that we would cut them in half. Then he raised his finger to the sky meaning he could take us on all by himself. Then I gave him an onion to tell him that he would soon taste the bitter tears of defeat and death. But he ate the onion in defiance! Then he showed me an egg to tell me how fragile our position is. There must be others close by. Let's get out of here."

Lars Ray related to this story of miscommunication. "I am about to complete a two-year assignment here in Mexico City for my company," he wrote. He knows only a little Spanish, and though many people he works with speak English well, there are still problems. "There have been many moments of confusion, misunderstandings, and flat out communication mishaps all due to the various levels of comprehension of words and their meanings—such as illustrated in your story. . . . That has been my experience here too . . . and man have I learned a lot from them!"[1] What pastor and activist Jesse Giglio says is true: "The greatest problem in communication is the illusion that it has been accomplished."[2]

WHAT MAKES PEOPLE LISTEN?

If you want to be a better communicator or a better leader, you can't depend on dumb luck. You must learn to connect with others by making the most of whatever skills and experience you have. When I listen to great communicators, I notice that there are a handful of factors they seem to draw upon that cause people to listen to them. As you read about them, think about which of them you could use to connect with others:

RELATIONSHIPS—WHO YOU KNOW

Why did millions of people start listening to Dr. Phil McGraw, a psychologist who helped lawyers as a trial consultant, and begin taking his advice on life, love, and relationships? For the same reason that millions started listening to Dr. Mehmet Oz about health issues. Both men knew Oprah Winfrey and appeared on her television show.

Certainly these two men have credentials. McGraw has a PhD in psychology, and Oz is a cardiothoracic surgeon and Columbia University professor. But most people neither know nor care about these facts. As soon as Oprah Winfrey's followers learned *she* had confidence in them, *they* had confidence in them.

One of the quickest ways to gain credibility with an individual, a group, or an audience is to borrow it from someone who already has credibility with them. It's the basis of sales referrals and word-of-mouth advertising. "Who" you know can open the door for you to connect with someone. Of course, once the door is open, you still have to deliver!

INSIGHT—WHAT YOU KNOW

Most people want to improve their situation in life. When they find someone who can communicate something of value, they will usually listen. If what they learn really helps, a sense of connection between them can often quickly develop.

> *Most people want to improve their situation in life. When they find someone who can communicate something of value to them, they will usually listen.*

One of the figures from American history whom I most admire is Benjamin Franklin. He had a remarkable career and is responsible as one of our Founding Fathers for the success of our nation. Franklin had little formal education—he attended school only two years—yet he was highly respected because of his knowledge and keen insight. A voracious reader and intellectually curious man, he became an expert in a remarkable number of areas: printing and publishing, politics, civic activism, the sciences, and diplomacy. He was an innovative inventor, secured the support of France during the Revolutionary War, founded the first public library in America, served as the first president of the American Philosophical Society, and helped draft the Declaration of Independence. Walter Isaacson called Franklin "the most accomplished American of his age." He was highly influential, and the people of his time felt a sense of connection with him when he shared his wisdom.

If you have an area of expertise and generously share it with others, you give people reasons to respect you and develop a sense of connection with you.

SUCCESS—WHAT YOU HAVE DONE

A lot of people ask me how I got my start as a speaker outside of a local church. They want to know what my marketing strategy was and how I was able to break in. The truth is that I didn't have a plan to become that kind of speaker. People became aware of the success I was having in leading and growing a church, and they began inviting me to speak on the subject. They wanted to hear what I had to say because of what I had done.

America has a success culture. People want to be successful, and they seek out others who have accomplished something to get their advice. If you are successful in anything you do, there will be people who will want to listen to you. I think many people assume that if someone can succeed in an area, he or she possesses knowledge that may be valuable to them in their own endeavors. And if the person's success is in the same area as theirs, the potential for connection is even stronger.

ABILITY—WHAT YOU CAN DO

Individuals who perform at a high level in their profession often have instant credibility with others. People admire them, they want to be like them, and they feel connected to them. When they speak, others listen—even if the area of their skill has nothing to do with the advice they give.

Think about Michael Jordan. He has made more money from endorsements than he ever did playing basketball. Is it because of his knowledge of the products he endorses? No. It's because of what he can do with a basketball. The same can be said of Olympic swimmer Michael Phelps. People listen to him because of what he can do in the pool. And when an actor tells us we should drive a certain car, we don't listen because of his expertise on engines. We listen because we admire his talent. Excellence connects. If you possess a high level of ability in an area, others may desire to connect with you because of it.

SACRIFICE—HOW YOU HAVE LIVED

Mother Teresa had the respect and the ear of leaders around the world. People of all faiths seemed to admire her. Why was that? Why did they listen to her—a poor, diminutive schoolteacher who lived in the slums in India? Because of the life of sacrifice she lived.

I think our hearts naturally go out to people who have sacrificed or suffered. Consider the feelings of sympathy and connection that people felt for the firefighters who served in New York City during the 9/11 attacks on the World Trade Center Towers. Notice how much respect is given to the families of servicemen and service-women who died while in Iraq and Afghanistan. Think about the weight that is given to the words of civil rights leaders who helped to pave the way for the election of Barack Obama, the United States' first African-American president.

If you have made sacrifices, suffered tragedy, or overcome painful obstacles, many people will relate to you. And if you have been able to remain positive yet humble in the midst of life's difficulties, others will admire you and be able to connect with you.

These five connection factors are just the beginning. I'm sure you can think of other reasons people connect. The point is that you must take whatever you have and use it to connect with others. The more factors you have and the better you become at using them, the greater your chance of connecting with people. You must play to your strengths, develop your own style, and cultivate whatever skills you can in order to connect with people.

THE ART OF CONNECTING
BY CHARLIE WETZEL

One of the questions people ask me all the time is, "What's John really like?" I'm glad that I can tell you that the John Maxwell I've observed in private for a decade and a half is the same as the one everyone sees in front of an audience. I've seen him in hundreds of situations—speaking in an arena with thousands of people, preaching in churches, teaching leadership lessons to a dozen people, attending meetings, negotiating deals, spending time with his family, traveling on the road, and simply having fun. And I can tell you, he genuinely practices what he teaches. And he always connects.

I'll be honest with you. The first time I saw John speak at his church, I was skeptical about him. He just seemed a little bit too slick in his preaching. He walked onto the stage well groomed, wearing a nice suit, relaxed, and smiling. He had an easy confidence—as if he were talking to friends he'd known for years. Now that I think about it, I guess he was.

That experience was not what I was accustomed to. I grew up attending a church with about thirty-five people in a service; there were one thousand in the auditorium in the service at John's church. I was used to a choir of eight people and the accompaniment of a poorly played organ; the music at his church was of professional quality. My childhood pastor was a stern, introverted engineer who had recently become a minister; John was a communicator who had

---

honed his speaking skills for twenty-five years. Let's just say I needed to adjust my expectations. Fortunately, it took only a few weeks for me to recognize that John was genuine, not a phony. And I quickly realized that what he was teaching every week was helping me and really making a difference in my life.

I'll admit, my current view of John is not entirely unbiased. I'm grateful to him for many things. However, I think my observations are genuine and accurate. Outside of his family, there are not a lot of people who know him much better than I do. And because I'm an observer by nature—as all writers are—I think I can identify what makes John tick as a communicator in front of an audience, one-on-one, and even in writing. Here's what I can tell you.

CONNECTING WITH A LIVE AUDIENCE

The first five years I worked with John, I was a student of communication. I spent a lot of time studying his communication style with an audience. Before becoming a writer, I was a teacher. And I think I was a pretty good one. My strength is communicating complex information simply, quickly, and practically. But I wasn't skilled at captivating an audience the way John does, and it usually took me weeks of speaking to a class of students before I began to connect with them. I watched John because I wanted to learn. I also had access to other great communicators, and I learned from them as well. What I discovered is that John, like all of the communicators I greatly admire, exhibits five qualities:

He Possesses Great Confidence. I have yet to observe a great communicator who didn't possess confidence. As I already mentioned, I at first found John's confidence a little off-putting because of the environment in which he was speaking. But that was really because of my personal baggage. The reality is that it's difficult to connect with and enjoy speakers who are uncertain. Their doubts about themselves make you doubt them, and that becomes a distraction. It becomes impossible to settle in and be at ease as a listener because their lack of certainty brings up questions concerning their credibility. Either consciously or subconsciously, you're continually asking yourself, "Is that really true?" When a speaker doesn't say something with conviction, we remain unconvinced.

If you desire to be a good communicator and to connect with your audience, you need to do the work required to gain confidence. That may be as difficult as working through personal issues related to your past, as simple as wearing the right clothes when speaking, or as mundane as getting more experience in front of an audience by doing more speaking. No matter what's required, put in the work—for great communicators possess great confidence.

He Exhibits Authenticity. The thing that won me over to John in those early weeks of hearing him speak was his authenticity. He wasn't pretending to be anything other than who he was. Like anybody else, he has his weaknesses as well as his strengths, but he's willing to admit both.

> *"Great communicators possess great confidence."*
>
> —CHARLIE WETZEL

As I've gotten to know him personally, I can tell you that John doesn't believe his own press. He's pleased when people tell him that he's helped them, but it's in a spirit of gratitude and a sense that he's fulfilling his purpose. I once heard singer George Michael talk about fame in an interview with Chris Cuomo on *Good Morning America*. Michael said, "You've got to understand, I don't inhale any of that. It's dangerous."[3] That also describes John's attitude.

One of the dangers of studying communicators is falling into the trap of trying to imitate them. What a mistake. Early on, I

> *"To connect with people, be yourself, at your best."*
>
> —CHARLIE WETZEL

wanted to be more like John in my speaking, but all that did was intimidate me and cause me to lose confidence. It took me several years of speaking to find my voice and rhythm again. I can't be like John. I'm not "larger than life." He fills the room with his personality, whether that's a living room or a stadium. I don't. Instead, my goal is to speak genuinely in my own voice. To connect with people, be yourself, at your best. That's something anyone can learn to do.

He Prepares Thoroughly. I've never seen John unready to speak to an audience. He's already told you about some of his preparation when it comes to learning what his host wants and knowing about his audience, so I'll tell you about the other things he does.

John is a meticulous outliner. With his experience and personality, he could easily wing it, but he never does. He prepares. He writes out every bullet point. He includes every quote and story in his outline. Because he reads voraciously and is constantly filing quotes and illustrations, he always has a lot of material ready to include in any message he's writing. (You could say he's always preparing because he's always learning and researching.) He writes his outlines by hand with a four-color Bic pen, tapes his quotes into his outline, and reminds himself about personal stories by writing a word or two preceded by an asterisk.

What's more, John is prepared even when others don't expect him to be. Whenever he travels, he carries about a dozen laminated cards with him, each with an outline for a speech that he could give at a moment's notice. When we were on a book tour several years ago, at one of the stops where he was getting ready to communicate, someone who had heard him speak there a year before mentioned how much he had enjoyed John's talk. That previous talk was very similar to what John was speaking about on the book tour. In a flash John pulled out one of his cards and spoke on a different subject. Nobody but John, me, and another traveling companion had any idea, because John didn't skip a beat.

> *"Rare is the communicator who is able to connect with people without using humor."*
>
> —CHARLIE WETZEL

He Utilizes Humor. John is funny on the stage and off of it. He loves a good joke. He has a fast mind and a quick wit. And he easily laughs at himself. When he looks for material to file, humor is one of the things he seeks.

What sometimes amazes me is how corny John can be. He can say things and tell stories onstage that nobody else in the world could get away with. Do you want to know how? He does it because he genuinely thinks it's funny. And trust me, nobody likes to have a good time more than John does.

Rare is the communicator who is able to connect with people without using humor. I'm sure there are some, but honestly I can't think of any. The key is to stick with what you find funny and not to force it.

He Focuses on Others. John has already written an entire chapter on how connecting is about others, not ourselves. And if you've ever heard him speak, then you know that from the moment he arrives somewhere to speak, he's thinking about the people he will talk to. If he can, he meets and greets people beforehand. And when he begins his presentation, he speaks positively about his host or talks about someone he knows or has met in the audience. And when he's done, he hangs around to greet people, shake hands, and sign books.

As I prepared to work on this chapter, I got in touch with people to get their insight into how John has connected with them. One of those people was Marty Grunder. He recounted an experience with John that illustrates how John does this. Marty said,

> Five years ago, John only knew of me because I had sent him a copy of my book (for which, by the way, he sent me a nice handwritten thank you note). When he was getting ready to speak in Dayton, Ohio, he asked Linda Eggers, his assistant, to call me and invite me to attend. During the session, he called me out of the audience to recognize me in front of my hometown crowd. I knew several people in the gathering of thousands and needless to say, they were flabbergasted I knew John. He also made sure I sat next to him at lunch. He talked to me and looked me right in the eye, like I was the only one in the room. You can imagine how I felt!

This others-mindedness is a hallmark of John's life. He possesses an uncanny ability to create special moments and to honor people. And he doesn't just do it off the cuff. I've watched him plan something special a year in advance. He'll spend months figuring out what will make a moment special for someone. I've seen him honor Bill Bright, Billy Graham, Elmer Towns, Orval Butcher, his father, and others. He has great timing and an incredible sense of the moment.

I have also been the recipient of one of these special moments. Every month John used to teach a one-hour leadership lesson to his staff, which was recorded and then sent by subscription to more than ten thousand people. I'll never forget the day John was teaching a lesson called "Searching for Eagles," in which he explained what to look for in a potential leader. I had been working for him only a few months. At the end of that lesson he said, "I want to tell you about an eagle who has just come to work with me." He then proceeded to say many nice things about me and tell a story about something I had done for him on my own initiative.

That may not sound like much, but I think it was the first time I had been singled out publicly for my work. My wife was in the room at the time! So was the president of John's company and his entire staff. And thousands of people across the country were going to hear him praise me. It made me cry. Even today as I think about it—more than a decade later—it makes me tear up. It was unexpected, he didn't have to do it, and he said it from his heart. I've felt a connection to John ever since. He really does care about people, and he goes out of his way to show it.

CONNECTING ONE-ON-ONE

Over the years, I've met a lot of speakers and celebrities. Some of them find it easy to be charming, entertaining, and engaging onstage, but once they step off the platform, they have a difficult time relating to others. That's not the case with John. In my opinion, he's actually better with people one-on-one than he is with a large audience. He really understands people and wants to help them. More than anything else, I think his strength on the stage comes from those qualities. Singer-songwriter Carole King says, "It's all about connections. I want to connect with people; I want people to think, 'Yeah, that's how I feel.' And, if I can do that, that's an accomplishment." John does that on the stage, in a group, and one-on-one.

> *"It's all about connections. I want to connect with people; I want people to think, 'Yeah, that's how I feel.' And, if I can do that, that's an accomplishment."*
> —CAROLE KING

111

It's hard to decide which things to tell you about my personal interaction with John. I could describe how he upgraded me to first class on the first trip I took with him and how he fixed a bagel for my breakfast as we talked—not a big deal, but pretty unusual for the CEO to do for a new employee. Or I could tell you about the time he wanted to send me to a writers' conference, but to attend I would have missed my first wedding anniversary. His solution was to pay for me and my wife to go together. Or I could let you know that he was the first person to call me and see how I was doing after my mother died.

Everyone around John could tell you similar kinds of stories. All I can say is that he has always made me feel like a friend, not an employee. And if you're familiar with his book *25 Ways to Win with People*, I can assure you that he actually does all of those things all the time. The book is a course on connecting with others one-on-one, and John lives it every day.

But none of those stories actually helps you, so I'll tell you about one thing that John always does that helps him connect with others that you can easily learn to do. I call it intentional inclusion. He makes people feel welcome and wanted, and he invites them into experiences they might not otherwise have. When John attends a meeting, he not only includes the people needed for it, he also invites someone who will learn and grow from the experience. When he gets season tickets for a sports team or buys tickets to a show, he always gets enough so that he can take others with him. He introduces people to others so that they can build connections. For example, Anne Beiler of Auntie Ann's Pretzels had always wanted to meet Truett Cathy, the founder of Chick-fil-A, so John invited both of them to dinner at his home.

John continually looks for ways to add value to people. And he tries to make everything fun for the people around him. Once while

I was on a trip with John, we got to ride in a limousine while receiving an unexpected police escort to the airport. John was having the time of his life. And what did he do? He pulled out his cell phone and called Linda Eggers, his assistant, who hadn't been able to travel with us. He told Linda all about it while it was happening so that she could share the moment.

If you did nothing else but intentionally include others in your best experiences and favorite things, you would become a much better connector overnight.

CONNECTING THROUGH THE WRITTEN WORD

After listening to hundreds of speakers and authors, I've come to the conclusion that there are two kinds of people in the world of communication: there are speakers who write and writers who speak. I have yet to meet someone who does both at the highest level.

"Which is John?" you may ask. In my opinion, he is a speaker who writes. First and foremost, John shines in front of an audience. He connects because he knows exactly what everyone is thinking, and he knows how to say just the right thing in the right tone of voice to set the audience at ease, to make people laugh, or to touch everyone's heart. But unlike some speakers who just make the crowd enjoy the moment, John can deliver great ideas. In fact, when people meet me and find out I write for John, they often say something like, "What? You mean John takes credit for your ideas?"

"No," I explain. "John is the idea guy. He'll never live long enough to share all the ideas he has. No, I just take his ideas and wordsmith them so that people will want to read them in written form." That's a different skill from interacting with an audience.

Like most great communicators, John conveys an incredible amount of meaning through inflection, facial expressions, timing, and body language. That comes naturally to him onstage. Many speakers have a hard time communicating at the same level through the written word. John can write, but he's a speaker first.

So how is he able to connect in writing? I'm going to let you in on a little secret that I've never heard any other writer talk about. When I work on John's books, I don't try to say exactly what he would say the way he would say it. In fact, I can tell when books have been created from a speaker's transcripts. They fall flat and they don't work. Why? Because they are missing all of what a great communicator includes nonverbally. So what I do is take John's ideas and try to create the same response in a reader that John would get if he were conveying it personally. I try to make readers feel the same thing they feel when they see John in person. In other words, my task is to make sure his ideas connect.

BECOMING A CONNECTING COMMUNICATOR
IS A PROCESS

I hope you found Charlie's observations helpful. To be honest, one of my concerns about including them in this book is that it may appear to be self-serving. I hope that wasn't the case. But to put things in proper perspective, I want to tell you a story that will help you understand how bad I was as a communicator when I started out. I think it's the kind of thing that can give anyone hope.

While I was in college studying for the ministry, it was common for small churches to invite potential pastors to speak to their congregation. One week before I was to preach my first message of that type, I accompanied a friend named Don so I could hear his first attempt.

Don got up before the congregation and launched in. But after only three minutes, he ran out of gas. He had nothing more to say. After a few moments of stammering, he quickly sat down. Everyone was in shock.

On the drive back to campus, the one thing I kept telling myself was, "My sermon has to be longer than three minutes." The rest of that week I spent every spare second preparing for my inaugural speech. As I worked, I kept adding points to my outline. By Sunday, I had nine points. I didn't give a single thought to connecting with my audience. I had only one goal: to last longer than three minutes.

Margaret and I were engaged at that time, and she accompanied me to the little church for this important first step in my career. When I was done with the sermon, I was pleased with myself and felt satisfied. I thought I had done a pretty good job.

On the drive back to town, Margaret was unusually silent. Finally, I asked her, "How did I do this morning?"

"I think you did fine for your first time," she responded after some hesitation. She didn't sound very enthusiastic, but I was encouraged nonetheless.

"How long did I speak?"

After a really long pause, she replied, "Fifty-five minutes."

I was clueless! Can you imagine what the people must have thought as they left the service? I had no idea how long and boring my message had been. And they knew that I didn't know. But what could they do? Too polite to simply walk out, they were held captive by an inexperienced speaker who had no idea how to communicate. They would have preferred three-minute Don.

Philosopher-poet Ralph Waldo Emerson said, "All great speakers were bad speakers first." Those words certainly applied to me. I started off bad—really bad. It took me many years of practice to improve my speaking. And I got better only after I learned what all good communicators have in common: they connect.

I don't know what your goals are or what your potential is as a communicator. I don't know what dreams you possess. But I can tell you this. You are more likely to achieve them if you become an effective communicator, and that comes from being a great connector. Max De Pree, author of *Leadership Is an Art*, asserts, "There may be no single thing more important in our efforts to achieve meaningful work and fulfilling relationships than to learn to practice the art of communication." I couldn't agree more.

> *"All great speakers were bad speakers first."*
>
> —RALPH WALDO EMERSON

If you want to have better relationships, if you want to achieve personal success, or if you want to become a better leader, make connecting your goal. To do that, become a student of communication if you aren't one already. Study effective and ineffective speakers, observing what works and what doesn't. Give thought to what causes people to listen to others, and begin working on cultivating those characteristics. And wherever you go, watch how good connectors interact with people one-on-one. You can become better at connecting if you're willing to work at it.

CONNECTING WITH PEOPLE AT ALL LEVELS

CONNECTING PRINCIPLE: Connecting is more skill than natural talent.

KEY CONCEPT: The skills you learn to connect at one level can be used to start connecting at the next level.

CONNECTING ONE-ON-ONE

Most people believe that it's easier to connect with people one-on-one than with a group or an audience. I believe that's usually true because they have more practice connecting with an individual than they do with a group. The way to overcome the fear of speaking to larger groups is to practice using the skills you acquire at one level on the next level. The process begins with using whatever gifts and talents you possess to begin connecting with people one-on-one.

To connect well one-on-one, you need to:

- Have interest in the person.

- Place value on that person.

- Put his or her interests ahead of your own.

- Express gratitude to and for that person.

CONNECTING IN A GROUP

Once you have begun to connect well one-on-one, take stock of what skills you've developed and what assets you've utilized to succeed in that arena. Now consider how you can use these things to connect in a group. What easily transfers? What must be "translated" or altered in some way to be used with a group? Use those skills. In addition, take the four things mentioned above for connecting one-on-one and expand them to apply to a group:

- Show interest in each person in your group. Do this by asking each person questions.

- Place value on each person by pointing out his or her value to the others in the group.

- Make it your goal to add value to everyone in the group, and let them know that is your intention.

- Express your gratitude to each person in front of others.

CONNECTING WITH AN AUDIENCE

As you become more adept at connecting with groups, once again take stock of what worked in connecting with them. Try to anticipate what could work well with larger audiences. Just remember: the larger the audience, the more energy you need to bring to your communication.

To start the connection process, do the following:

- Show interest in your audience. When possible, meet and greet audience members before you speak. While speaking, let people know that you understand that each person is unique and special.

- Place value on each person by letting them know you spent a lot of time preparing your talk because you value them, their purpose, and their time.

- Put the people first by letting them know you are there to serve them. I do this by being willing to answer questions, making myself available to inter-

act with people after a speech, and being available
to sign books.

• Express gratitude to them and thank them for
their time.

PART II

CONNECTING PRACTICES

6

CONNECTORS CONNECT ON COMMON GROUND

If I had to pick a first rule of communication—the practice above all others that opens the door to connection with others—it would be to look for common ground. That rule applies whether you're resolving conflict with your spouse, teaching a child, negotiating a deal, selling a product, writing a book, leading a meeting, or communicating to an audience.

I've already explained how, in the first several years of my career as a leader and speaker, my focus was too much on myself. And only when I started to realize that connecting is all about others did I start to improve. It's difficult to find common ground with others when the only person you're focused on is yourself!

> *It's difficult to find common ground with others when the only person you're focused on is yourself!*

I think you begin to understand others better when you understand yourself, but to grow to another level, you have to work at understanding others. I experienced another *aha* moment that helped me connect with others when I read Florence Littauer's book *Personality Plus*. For the first time I recognized that different temperaments caused people to think and act differently than I do. That may seem obvious to you, but it was an important eye opener for me. More importantly, I realized that there is no one right temperament. To be honest, for years I thought my choleric temperament was superior to all others. As a result, I tried to convert people with other temperaments to mine. How ridiculous! I was like the lady who was disappointed with the result of her husband's eye surgery. She told her friend, "We spent over $4,000 on laser surgery for his eyes, and he still can't see things from my point of view!"[1]

I continue to work at learning how others think and perceive the world. Recently I read a book by Terry Felber called *Am I Making Myself Clear?* He says that people have different representational systems based on the five senses, which provide the primary basis for their thoughts and feelings. For example, if several people walked down the beach together, their recollections of the experience would be very different based on their representational system. One might remember how the sun felt on his skin and the sand on his feet. Another might remember the look of the water and the vivid colors of the sunset. The third might be able to describe the sounds of the ocean and birds, and another the smell of the salt air and the tanning lotion of nearby sunbathers. Each of us creates a framework for the way we process information. Felber says, "If you can learn to pinpoint how those around you experience the world, and really try to experience the same world they do, you'll be amazed at how effective your communication will become."[2] That's simply another way to look for common ground.

BARRIERS TO FINDING COMMON GROUND

People who connect are always searching for common ground. That probably seems obvious because all positive relationships are built on common interests and values. They build upon agreement, not disagreement. But if that's true, why do so many people neglect to search for common ground and build upon it? There are many reasons, but I will give you what I believe to be the top four barriers to finding common ground. You must guard against them:

1. ASSUMPTION—"I ALREADY KNOW WHAT OTHERS KNOW, FEEL, AND WANT"

Jerry Ballard says, "All miscommunications are the result of differing assumptions." Haven't you found that to be true? Sometimes the results are tragic. Often they can be comical, as was the case for a traveler between flights at an airport. She went to a lounge and bought a small package of cookies and then sat down to read a newspaper.

> *"All miscommunications are the result of differing assumptions."*
>
> —JERRY BALLARD

She became aware of a rustling noise and looked to see a neatly dressed man helping himself to the cookies. She didn't want to make a scene, so she leaned over and took a cookie herself, hoping he would get the message. As time passed, she thought she had been successful. But then she heard more rustling. She couldn't believe it. He was helping himself to another cookie!

There was only one cookie left. While she watched in disbelief, the man broke the remaining cookie in two, pushed half across to her, popped the other half into his mouth, and left.

The traveler was still furious some time later when her flight was announced. When she opened her handbag to get her ticket, imagine how shocked and embarrassed she was when she looked there and found her pack of unopened cookies![3]

Like the woman in the story, didn't you assume that the man was helping himself to her cookies? That's what I thought the first time I read the story. And that tells us a lot about ourselves. Too often I have been guilty of making assumptions about people. I have often made generalizations when I should have been making observations. It is easy to label people and then see them only in that light.

We need to remember that all generalizations are false, including this one. Once a person has been placed neatly within a certain box, it becomes more difficult for us to think of him or her as being anything different. Instead, we need to be like a good tailor. Every time he sees a client, he takes new measurements. He never assumes people are the same as the last time he saw them.

It's unwise to make assumptions about others, even if they're close to you. Deb Ingino, founder and president of mywiredstyle.com, told me about a young single mother from a parenting workshop she taught, who made assumptions when it came to her son. The mother often told her son that he was just like his father. The problem was that the boy's father was in jail, and the mother often said negative things about the man. She assumed that her son knew that she loved him and that she was speaking about his personality traits. But her comments were having a negative effect on the boy, so she changed her interaction and became intentional in the way she connected with him. "Now," said Deb, "she seeks to discover what he knows, she nurtures his strengths, encourages him in those strengths, and is seeing a remarkable improvement in his behavior and their relationship."[4]

Do you make assumptions about people—based on their background, profession, race, gender, age, nationality, politics, faith, or other factors? Whenever you are quick to do that, you stop paying attention to people and miss clues that would otherwise help you to find and reach common ground with them. Nigerian writer Chimamanda Adichie says, "If we hear only a single story about another person or country, we risk a critical misunderstanding."[5] Why? Because we may assume that it tells the whole story about that person or country, and we close our minds to learning more about them. When that happens, it becomes difficult to find common ground.

2. ARROGANCE—"I DON'T NEED TO KNOW WHAT OTHERS KNOW, FEEL, OR WANT"

Arrogant people seldom meet others on common ground. Why? Because they don't make the effort—they believe they shouldn't have to. In their estimation, they live on higher ground than others. They don't want to lower themselves to other people's level. They expect everyone else to make the effort to come to them.

One of the secrets of getting along with others is taking into consideration other people's views. Supreme Court Justice Louis D. Brandeis observed, "Nine-tenths of the serious controversies that arise in life result from misunderstanding, from one man not knowing the facts which to the other man seem important, or otherwise failing to appreciate his point of view."

Most of us are willing to admit, as the Beatles did, that we need a little help from our friends. We know how ridiculous it is for someone to think they have all the answers. Such people seem hopelessly out-of-date. They're like Archie Bunker in the classic 1970s sitcom *All in the Family*. Opinionated, narrow-minded, and bigoted, Bunker

> *You can't build a relationship with everybody in the room when you don't care about anybody in the room.*

expected everyone to meet him on his own terms. Friends and family alike were exposed to his insults. Poor Edith, his wife, usually got the worst of it. "Our problem, Edith," he told her on one occasion, "is that I talk in English, and you hear in Dingbat."

Bunker was such a caricature that he made audiences laugh. It's not as funny when someone displays such arrogance in real life. I've studied leaders and communicators for more than forty years, and what's sad is that most people try to build a case for their competence or their viewpoint when they communicate. As a result, they seldom connect because there is an arrogance about them that builds a barrier between them and others. You can't build a relationship with everybody in the room when you don't care about anybody in the room.

3. INDIFFERENCE—"I DON'T CARE TO KNOW WHAT OTHERS KNOW, FEEL, OR WANT"

Comedian George Carlin joked, "Scientists announced today that they had found a cure for apathy. However, they claim no one has shown the slightest bit of interest in it." That can be said of some people when they communicate. They may not feel superior to their listeners, but they don't go out of their way to learn about them either. Maybe that's because it simply takes a lot of work.

Each year I travel internationally as part of my speaking schedule. I find it very challenging. There are often language barriers and always cultural ones to overcome. I'm constantly thinking about ways to connect by finding common ground for these events, and it always requires a lot of preparation.

Many years ago Margaret and I took our children, Joel Porter and Elizabeth, to Russia. At the time, the country was in transition with the fall of the Soviet Union. I was given an important speaking engagement within the Kremlin, and as I prepared for it, I wracked my brain trying to think of ways to connect with my audience. Then it hit me: our daughter, Elizabeth, has a wonderful voice and was looking for an opportunity to sing to the people in Russian.

Elizabeth practiced long and hard learning phonetically to sing a song. At the event when she got up to sing, the audience came to life as soon as they heard Russian words coming out of her mouth. The energy in the room intensified immediately. And when she was finished, their applause was deafening! It meant a lot to them that she had made the effort to connect with them in their language. What former South African president Nelson Mandela said is true: "If you talk to a man in the language he understands, that goes to his head. If you talk to him in his language, that goes to his heart."

The bottom line is that indifference is really a form of selfishness. Communicators who are indifferent are focused on themselves and their own comfort instead of on extending themselves and finding the best way to relate to others.

If you have had a hard time connecting with people because you haven't made the effort to get to know them, then heed the words of English novelist George Eliot, who said, "Try to care about something in this vast world besides the gratification of small selfish desires. Try to care for what is best in thought and action—something that is good apart from the accidents of your own lot. Look on other lives besides your own. See what their troubles are, and how they are borne." Most people appreciate any effort you make, no matter how small, to see things from their point of view.

4. Control—"I Don't Want Others to Know What I Know, Feel, or Want"

Finding common ground is a two-way street. While it's important to focus on others to understand them, it's also critical to be open and authentic so that others understand you. Of course, not all leaders and communicators are willing to do this. As author and former U.S. Navy captain Mike Abrashoff observes, "Some leaders feel that by keeping people in the dark, they maintain a measure of control. But that is a leader's folly and an organization's failure. Secrecy spawns isolation, not success. Knowledge is power, yes, but what leaders need is collective power, and that requires collective knowledge. I found that the more people knew what the goals were, the better buy-in I got—and the better results we achieved together."[6] As C. Hannan points out, if you go the next step, results can be even better. Hannan says, "If you explain why and the reason behind it and for it, it not only helps others to understand the purpose but it also allows them to buy into the vision and be a part if it. Then you can work together!"[7]

> "We the uninformed, working for the inaccessible, are doing the impossible for the ungrateful!"
>
> —THE SUBORDINATE'S LAMENT
> BY JIM LUNDY

Anytime that employees sense that information is being kept from them and that they do not have a part in achieving the organization's goals, they feel like outsiders. As a result, their morale drops, and so does their performance. Likewise, when audience members sense that a speaker is holding back or prides himself or herself on being on the "inside" but doesn't include the audience, people feel alienated.

I love Jim Lundy's take on this in his

book *Lead, Follow, or Get Out of the Way.* In it, he includes the response of people who work in an environment where leaders hold back from them. He writes about the "Subordinate's Lament," which says, "We the uninformed, working for the inaccessible, are doing the impossible for the ungrateful!"[8] And the "Mushroom Farm Lament" goes like this: "We feel we're being kept in the dark. Every once in a while someone comes around and spreads manure on us. When our heads pop up, they're chopped off. And then we're canned."[9]

Good leaders and communicators don't isolate themselves, and they don't deliberately keep people in the dark. They inform people, make them a part of what's going on, and include them in decision making whenever possible. You cannot establish common ground if you refuse to let anyone know who you are or what you believe.

CULTIVATING A COMMON GROUND MIND-SET

Most people believe that finding common ground with others is a matter of talent: some people are simply good connectors while others aren't. While I do agree that not everyone starts out with the same ability to connect, I also believe that anyone can learn to connect better because *connecting is a choice.* It is a mind-set that can be learned. If you want to increase your odds of connecting with others, then make the following choices every day of your life:

> *Connecting is a choice.*

AVAILABILITY—"I WILL CHOOSE TO SPEND TIME WITH OTHERS"

Common ground must be discovered, and that takes time. Someone once told me that the typical business executive in the United

States has an on-the-job attention span of only six minutes. That's pathetic. In six minutes a person can hardly get his feet on the ground, much less find common ground.

Availability also requires intentionality. Hans Schiefelbein wrote, "When I was in charge of large group events, I would often stay close to people in production or be running around like I was the director of a big-budget film. I wanted to look important, so I wasn't available. That may come from ego and may be different from finding common ground, but maybe it's a pull that leaders feel that takes them away from being available."[10]

As a leader and communicator, I have always made it my goal to be available to others. When I'm with friends or family, I don't disconnect; I stay engaged. When I am a speaker at a conference, I sign books and talk with people during breaks instead of resting. When I was a local church pastor, I had a rule on Sundays for myself and my staff: while the people were on-site, there were to be no closed-door meetings. I wanted my staff to walk slowly through the crowd and be available. I also was available. I greeted people, chatted with them, and listened to them. It not only helped me to connect with them one on one, but it also helped me to be focused on them by the time I spoke.

LISTENING—"I WILL LISTEN MY WAY TO COMMON GROUND"

When I was a child, I sometimes played the Hot or Cold game with my friends. If you're about my age, maybe you did too. Whoever was "it" left the room, and the other kids would hide some small object. When the person came back, his job was to find it. As he looked around, the other players would tell him if he was getting colder (moving away from the hidden object) or warmer (getting closer). When he got really close, someone would tell him, "You're red-hot. You're on fire!"

I believe that every day people are playing variations of the Hot or Cold game in their lives. They are seeking success, but they don't know where it is. They are looking for others who share common values, but they don't know how to find them. If you are a leader or communicator, you have an opportunity to help them in their search. But to do that, you need to learn to listen. How else will you know what they're looking for?

> *"Listening requires giving up our favorite human pastime— involvement in ourselves and our own self-interest."*
>
> —SONYA HAMLIN

Finding common ground requires us to pay attention to others. Sonya Hamlin, in her book, *How to Talk So People Listen*, notes that most people find this difficult because of the "Me-First Factor." She wrote: "Listening requires giving up our favorite human pastime—involvement in ourselves and our own self-interest. It's our primary, entirely human focus. And it's where our motivation to do anything comes from. With this as a base, can you see what a problem is created when we're asked to listen to someone else?"

What is her solution? "To make anyone listen while you try to get your message across," she recommends, "you must always answer the listener's instinctive question: 'Why should I listen to you? What's in it for me if I let you in?'" Anytime you are willing to listen to others and figure out how the thing you're offering fills their needs, you've found a way to reach common ground.

QUESTIONS—"I WILL BE INTERESTED ENOUGH IN OTHERS TO ASK QUESTIONS"

Peter Drucker, the father of modern management, remarked, "My greatest strength as a consultant is to be ignorant and ask a few questions." What a great way to find common ground. I've made it a practice in my speaking career to follow that advice. Whenever I am asked to speak to a company, I ask for a pre-call so that I can ask questions and find out more about them. Sometimes when I speak, I start my session by asking questions. Often I'll ask, "How many are from the business community? The educational community? Government? The religious community?" These questions not only help me to know my audience, but they also let people understand that I want to know them.

Television host Larry King, who has conducted thousands of interviews, says that asking questions is the secret of every good conversation. "I'm curious about everything," writes King in *How to Talk to Anyone, Anytime, Anywhere,* "and if I'm at a cocktail party, I often ask my favorite question: 'Why?' If a man tells me he and his family are moving to another city: 'Why?' A woman is changing jobs: 'Why?' Someone roots for the Mets: 'Why?' On my television show, I probably use this word more than any other. It's the greatest question ever asked, and it always will be. And it is certainly the surest way of keeping a conversation lively and interesting."

If you aren't especially outgoing or have a difficult time asking questions, you can use this trick that Duke Brekhus says he learned from Ron Puryear. Remember the word FORM, which stands for family, occupation, recreation, and message. Duke comments, "When we ask questions centered around these topics it is amazing how much we can learn about a person and how quickly we can get to know them."[11]

THOUGHTFULNESS—"I WILL THINK OF OTHERS AND LOOK FOR WAYS TO THANK THEM"

In the 1970s, I was the pastor of a fast-growing church in Lancaster, Ohio, where my days were filled with appointments and other demanding time commitments. Since we were understaffed, I often felt the crush of my schedule.

One day I noticed a name on my appointment calendar that in my estimation did not belong there. Although the man was a member of the church, he wasn't a leader, and I was trying to focus my attention on the top 20 percent of leaders at that time.

Impatiently, I asked my assistant what he wanted. When she responded that she wasn't sure, I became annoyed.

When Joe arrived at my office, I had one agenda—to get him in and out of my office as soon as possible.

"What can I do for you?" I asked as soon as he sat down.

"Nothing at all, Pastor," he answered to my surprise. "The question is, what can I do for you? I've been asking myself that question for the last several weeks, and when I finally came up with an answer, I set up this appointment. John, I can see that your schedule is full and you're very busy. I would like to run personal errands for you. If you can have a list of things you want me to do and give it to your assistant, I will stop by each Thursday afternoon and take care of them for you. Is that okay?"

I was shocked. I was also ashamed. What a thoughtful offer. For the next six years, Joe did errands for me every Thursday. He taught me a lot about finding common ground that day. And he became a friend for whom I am grateful. If you are able to show a similar kind of thoughtfulness, you will also find common ground with others.

OPENNESS—"I WILL LET PEOPLE INTO MY LIFE"

Recently I had the privilege of having dinner with former senator and Republican presidential nominee Bob Dole. We had an interesting discussion on leadership, politics, and world events. One of the things I mentioned to him that night was how impressed I was with the way his wife, Elizabeth Dole, handled her speaking responsibilities at the Republican convention in 1996. To everyone's surprise, she left the podium and walked into the audience, saying, "Now, you know tradition is that speakers at the Republican National Convention remain at this very imposing podium. But tonight I'd like to break with tradition for two reasons—one, I'm going to be speaking to friends. Secondly, I'm going to be speaking about the man I love. And it's just a lot more comfortable for me to be down here with you." Elizabeth Dole found a way to show her openness to people and created a sense of commonality with her audience.

Communication is all about the openness of finding commonality with others. In fact, the word *communication* comes from the Latin word *communis*, meaning "common."[12] Before we can communicate effectively, we must establish our commonness—the better we do that, the greater the potential for effective communication.

That's not easy for everyone. Michelle Pack understands the necessity. She says, "I will listen to others for hours, mainly because that is what people want more than anything—to be heard. However, due to a history of emotional abandonment, I shut down and do not share my heart with others. As one who writes and desires to communicate, this is my greatest wall to tear down."[13] Connection always requires *both* parties to engage and be open.

LIKABILITY—"I WILL CARE ABOUT PEOPLE"

Roger Ailes, a former communication consultant to presidents, believes the most influential factor in public speaking is likability. He says that if people like you, they will listen to you, and if they don't, they won't. So how does a person become likable? By caring about others. People like people who like them. When others know you care, they'll listen. The way I used to say it to my staff when I was a pastor is this: people don't care how much you know until they know how much you care.

> *People like people who like them.*

Grace Bower wrote to tell me a story about her daughter, Louise. When Louise was a teenage university student in Auckland, New Zealand, her friends Victoria and Phil had their first baby. Louise was very close to them and wanted to do something for them. She tried putting herself in their shoes, wondering what would be most helpful since they were first-time parents. She landed upon the idea of grocery shopping for them the first six weeks of baby Andrew's life.

Each week she picked up Victoria's shopping list and money, and off Louise would go to the store. Louise was also very attentive. When she noticed that important items were missing from the list, she would purchase them, knowing Victoria and Phil would need them. They were delighted, and they really sensed how much she cared about them. And two years later, when the couple had their second child, Louise once again did their shopping for them.[14] Who wouldn't love having a friend like that?

Think of your favorite teachers. I bet they were likable. Consider which neighbors you remember best from your childhood. Weren't they likable? How about your schoolmates or your relatives? What about your best boss? Chances are all of those people were likable! It's a highly attractive quality to possess, and it causes others to want to connect with you.

HUMILITY—"I WILL THINK OF MYSELF LESS SO I CAN THINK OF OTHERS MORE"

Poet, journalist, and editor Alan Ross asserted, "Humility means knowing and using your strength for the benefit of others, on behalf of a higher purpose. The humble leader is not weak, but strong . . . is not pre-occupied with self, but with how best to use his or her strengths for the good of others. A humble leader does not think less of himself, but chooses to consider the needs of others in fulfilling a worthy cause. I love to be in the presence of a humble leader because they bring out the very best in me. Their focus is on my purpose, my contribution, and my ability to accomplish all I set out to accomplish."[15] What a great perspective. False humility downplays one's genuine strengths to receive praise. Arrogance plays up one's strength to receive praise. Humility raises up others so they can be praised.

> *"Humility means knowing and using your strength for the benefit of others, on behalf of a higher purpose."*
>
> —ALAN ROSS

Many years ago I was invited to do the closing session for a three-day convention where many people would be speaking. For two days I sat in the audience and was bombarded by success stories. Every speaker was successful in family life, business, and the community. All the speakers shared stories of success in building companies and winning over people, and after a while, it seemed to me that each subsequent speaker was trying to "outsuccess" the previous one.

By the third day, I was overwhelmed and overloaded. I felt totally intimidated by these speakers. My track record, talent, experience, and results seemed insignificant compared to theirs. And I could tell that the audience felt as I did. They believed there was a huge gap between themselves and these speakers. Their morale was low, and I could tell they were feeling discouraged.

During the lunch break, I considered what I could do to turn things around. Someone needed to connect with the audience and close the gap. Suddenly, I knew what I needed to do. I threw out the speech I had prepared, and quickly began writing a new outline. It would be on failure, not success. I called it "Flops, Failures, and Fumbles." In it I included stories of my biggest blunders, my worst ideas, and my greatest failures as a leader. Everyone has been humbled by life at one time or another. That is where I would seek common ground.

When I got up to speak, I began by saying that I was overloaded on the subject of success and I sensed that perhaps they were too. For the next hour I shared with them my failings as a leader and a person. I admitted that I was surprised that my organization had done so well with me leading it. With each honest tale of failure, the audience and I moved closer together and found common ground. They related to me. They connected with my transparency. At the end of my session, I told them I believed in them, and the audience stood and cheered because they were so excited about their prospects for the future. They believed that if I could succeed, so could they.

If you want to impact people, don't talk about your successes; talk about your failures. Civil rights activist Cornel West says, "Humility means two things. One, a capacity for self-criticism. . . . The second feature is allowing others to shine, affirming others, empowering and enabling others. Those who lack humility are dogmatic and egotistical.

> *"Humility means two things. One, a capacity for self-criticism. . . . The second feature is allowing others to shine, affirming others, empowering and enabling others."*
>
> —CORNEL WEST

That masks a deep sense of insecurity. They feel the success of others is at the expense of their own fame and glory."

So how do you put these ideas into action? I recommend that you follow the advice of pastor and author Rick Warren, who advises that humility comes from:

- Admitting our weaknesses
- Being patient with others' weaknesses
- Being open to correction
- Pointing the spotlight at others

Do that with people, and they will relate to you and listen to what you have to say.

ADAPTABILITY—"I WILL MOVE FROM MY WORLD TO THEIRS"

Medieval scholar Thomas Aquinas asserted, "To convert somebody, go and take them by the hand and guide them." To move others, we must first be willing to move ourselves to where they are. We must adapt to others and try to see things from their point of view.

Henry J. Kaiser, a shipbuilder who revolutionized his industry in the 1940s, did this as well as he could for his time. He spent about two hundred thousand dollars one year on his phone bill so that he could spend hours every day connecting with his key executives across the country. Long before conference calls were commonplace, he arranged to have members of his staff in many locations all on the same call together. Maybe he couldn't physically move to his leaders' worlds every day, but he did the next best thing.

Joel Dobbs explained that in the work as an executive with a large Japanese company, he faced great difficulties in making connections with people in Japan. "The language and the culture are a minefield," Joel explained, "so one must be very careful in attempting to use anything more than the most basic of words. The relationships are further complicated by the fact that most of our work is conducted through translators making the interaction even more impersonal. I have found that sharing meals together and making a serious effort to try and enjoy some of the stranger foods that appear on the menu has gone a long way towards cementing relationships."[16]

Anytime you are aware of a gap between you and the people with whom you are trying to connect, it's wise to try to move to their world mentally, if not physically, and then search for something in your own background and experience that relates to theirs. That's what I did in the 1980s when my leadership and ministry were starting to receive recognition nationally. At that time, the Charles Fuller Institute was hosting a seminar called "Breaking the 200 Barrier" for pastors of smaller churches around the country. They invited me to teach those sessions, and I knew that would present a challenge. The church I led at that time had more than twenty-five hundred people in attendance. How could I relate to small church pastors when my congregation had thousands more people in it? More importantly, how could I help them relate to me?

I spent time thinking about their world, their challenges, and their dreams. And then it hit me: my church in Hillham would be our common ground. It was the smallest of churches, and it grew to more than two hundred under my leadership. I would show them how I grew my small church, and they would be able to relate to my experience and develop a game plan. That strategy worked. We connected in the sessions, they learned from my experience, and thousands of pastors went on to grow their churches.

Anytime you aren't sure about how to bridge the communication gap, don't start the process by telling people about yourself. Begin with moving to where they are and seeing things from their perspective. Adapt to them—don't expect them to adapt to you.

CONNECTORS GO FIRST

This willingness to see things from others' point of view is really the secret of finding common ground, and finding common ground is really the secret of connecting. If you were to do only this and nothing else, your communication would improve immensely in every area of your life. Because this is so important, I want to give you four pointers to help you become a better connector.

1. ASK, "DO I FEEL WHAT YOU FEEL?" BEFORE ASKING, "DO YOU FEEL WHAT I FEEL?"

Effective communication takes people on a journey. We cannot take others on that journey unless we start where they are. Only then can we connect and try to lead them where we want to take them.

Herb Kelleher, the founder of Southwest Airlines, was a master at this. He was in constant contact with the people who worked for the airline. He used to travel around the country, meeting and spending time with employees at every level of the organization, from executives to ticket agents and from flight attendants to baggage handlers. He knew how people felt because he went to where they worked, came alongside them, and experienced what they did. His attitude and actions created common ground and broke down barriers between employer and employee. No wonder the people who worked for him loved him and listened to him.

If you want to find common ground with others, the place to begin is with their feelings. If you can connect on an emotional level, connecting is much easier on every other level.

2. Ask, "Do I See What You See?" Before Asking, "Do You See What I See?"

For years as a leader and communicator, I was intent on people seeing what I saw. Vision casting came naturally to me, and I loved talking about what could be. Often when the organization wasn't moving forward as I wanted, I would think, *If others could see the future the way I see it, then we could move forward.* But the real problem was that I wanted others to see things my way first. Or worse, I assumed that they already saw everything from my perspective. Such misconceptions can lead to humbling and sometimes amusing results.

When Orville and Wilbur Wright succeeded in flying their plane at Kitty Hawk, North Carolina, on December 17, 1903, they sent a telegram to their sister in Dayton, Ohio, telling her of their great accomplishment. It read, "First sustained flight today fifty-nine seconds. Hope to be home by Christmas."

Their sister, excited by the news, rushed to the local newspaper office and gave the telegram to the editor so that he could report on it. The next morning, the newspaper headline that graced the paper said, "Popular Local Bicycle Merchants to be Home for Holidays!"

How could the editor miss the real news? He didn't see things as Orville and Wilbur's sister did. And she evidently didn't do anything to ensure that he did. Such a miscommunication seems comical to us today, but we're guilty of the same kinds of differences in perception. For example, in 2000 I attended my thirty-five-year class reunion for Circleville High School. I was very excited about it because it would be the first one I attended. I could hardly wait to get there. Imagine my surprise when I looked around and saw so many old people! I felt younger than everyone else looked. But I bet as they looked at me, they were surprised by how old I looked.

People can be in the same place sharing the same experience at the same time, but they can walk away from it having seen very different things. Good connectors understand this tendency and make an effort to see things from others' point of view first.

More than thirty years ago, it was my privilege to speak with Paul Rees at a leaders' conference. Known for his insight and wisdom, he was at that time in his eighties, and I was in my early thirties. During a Q&A session, someone asked if he could go back in his life and do something different, what would it be? I'll never forget his reply.

"If I could go back to my days as a young father," he responded, "I would work harder on seeing things through my children's eyes." He went on to explain that he had missed many teaching moments because he wanted his children to see what he saw first. That day I made a commitment to see through the eyes of others before I asked them to see from my perspective.

3. ASK, "DO I KNOW WHAT YOU KNOW?" BEFORE ASKING, "DO YOU KNOW WHAT I KNOW?"

For years as a leader and pastor, I attempted to help people work through relational conflicts. Most times when I get people in these situations to sit down together to communicate, their greatest desire is to express their point of view from their perspective. They want to make sure they get their point across. When the conflict is with me,

I usually let them talk until they "run out of gas," and then I ask them questions. Only after I know what they know, do I try to share my side of the story. The person who gives answers before understanding the problems is very foolish.

Abraham Lincoln said, "When I'm getting ready to reason with a man, I spend one-third of my time thinking about myself and what I am going to say—and two-thirds thinking about him and what he is going to say." If we want to find common ground, we would do well to do the same.

4. ASK, "DO I KNOW WHAT YOU WANT?" BEFORE ASKING, "DO YOU KNOW WHAT I WANT?"

Church leaders know that attendance typically changes in cycles. In most churches, attendance drops in the summer because people go on vacations, they want to spend more time in outdoor activities on the weekend, and they get tired because of the demands of parenthood while their children are out of school.

When I led a church, I would try to do something every year to keep the attendance up during the summer. After many futile attempts, I finally discovered an answer. One spring I shared with the congregation that during the summer I was going to speak on a series entitled, "You Asked for It." I encouraged every attendee to request the subject they would most like me to talk about, and I would pick the ten most requested topics. Thousands of people participated, we picked the top ten, and those became the sermon topics throughout the summer. The result was that attendance actually increased instead of decreasing. Why? Because I knew what people wanted to learn about.

Inventor Charles F. Kettering said, "There is a great deal of difference between knowing and understanding. You can know a lot

> *"There is a great deal of difference between knowing and understanding. You can know a lot about something and not really understand it."*
>
> —CHARLES F. KETTERING

about something and not really understand it." That can also be said about people. You can know a lot about a person and still not understand him or her. More information isn't always the answer. To really understand people, you must know what they want, and that requires you to go beyond the head and consider the heart.

When I want to really get to know someone, I ask three questions. People's answers to these give me great insight into someone's heart. The questions are:

- What do you dream about?

- What do you sing about?

- What do you cry about?

If you know the answers to those questions, you will be able to find common ground with someone and connect with that person.

If there is a more important key to communication than finding common ground, I certainly can't think of it. Common ground is the place where people can discuss differences, share ideas, find solutions, and start creating something together. Too often people see communication as the process of transmitting massive amounts of information to other people. But that's the wrong picture. As I already mentioned, communication is a journey. The more that people have in common, the better the chance that they can take that journey together.

CONNECTING WITH PEOPLE AT ALL LEVELS

CONNECTING PRACTICE: Connectors connect on common ground.

KEY CONCEPT: Know the reasons you and your listener want to communicate and build a bridge between those reasons.

CONNECTING ONE-ON-ONE

When two people come together to communicate, each of them has a reason for doing so. To connect on common ground, you must know your reason, know the other person's reason, and find a way to connect the two. The bottom line in finding common ground is knowing how to make the interaction a win for both parties.

Building a bridge on common ground is easier one-on-one than with many people because you can get immediate and continuous feedback from the other person. To find common ground, ask questions with an eye for common interests and experiences. When you find common ground, tell stories, share emotions, and offer lessons learned from those experiences. And if possible, do something together that you both enjoy.

CONNECTING IN A GROUP

Finding common ground in a group setting is a little more difficult because you can't focus on just a single person. (If you do, you risk losing the rest of the group.) So how do you do it? Begin by asking yourself, "What brought us together?" The answer to that question usually gives you an effective starting point.

If the group has been forced to come together, such as a mandatory committee designated by an employer, then ask yourself, "What is the one goal that all of us have?" With that goal in mind, acknowledge everyone's differences but also their ability to contribute to that common goal using their unique skills, reminding them that the goal is more important than the role. And when the group accomplishes a win, celebrate together.

CONNECTING WITH AN AUDIENCE

When people come to hear someone speak, their hope is to learn something that will help them. An anticipating audience has this first and foremost in their minds. A hostile audience may not be thinking about it, but if listening is to their advantage, they will be open to it. Tap into this desire to connect on common ground the next time you communicate in front of an audience. Use the following pattern: Feel, Felt, Found, Find.

- FEEL: Try to sense what they *feel* and acknowledge and validate their feelings.

- FELT: Share with them that you have also *felt* the same way.

- FOUND: Share with them what you *found* that has helped you.

- FIND: Offer to help them *find* help for their lives.

CONNECTORS DO THE DIFFICULT WORK OF KEEPING IT SIMPLE

A few years ago, I was being interviewed on a television talk show. The host held up a couple of my books and said, "John, I've read several of your books, and they are all so simple." His tone of voice, body language, and mannerisms made it clear to me and the audience that he did not mean it as a compliment!

My response was straightforward: "That's true. The principles in my books are simple to understand. But they are not always simple to apply." The audience applauded, and he conceded what I said was right.

WHAT'S WRONG WITH SIMPLE?

Ronnie Ding tells me that after a church service, the pastor shook hands with members of his congregation, and one of them commented on his sermon, saying "Pastor, you are smarter than Albert Einstein."

The pastor was surprised and flattered by that statement, but he didn't know how to respond. In fact, the more he thought about the comment, the more mystified he was by it. He couldn't sleep properly for a week!

The following Sunday, he finally asked the member what he meant by it.

"You see," the man responded, "Albert Einstein wrote something so difficult that only ten persons could understand him at that time. But when you preached, no one could understand you."[1]

I think a lot of people believe that if an individual, especially an author or speaker, bombards them with a lot of complex information or writes using big words in a style that is dense and difficult to understand, then he or she is somehow intelligent and credible. In the academic world, that seems to be especially true. When students can't understand their professor, they often assume it's because the professor is so smart and knows so much more than they do. I don't think that's always true. As real estate broker Sue Cartun commented, "If you use lengthy or stilted language to try to impress, you cannot connect. The audience is simply waiting for the torture to end."[2] Most often in such cases, the teacher isn't a good communicator. While educators often take something simple and make it complicated, communicators take something complicated and make it simple.

In his excellent book *The Power of Little Words*, author John Beckley, former business editor of *Newsweek*, observes: "The emphasis in education is rarely placed on communicating ideas simply and clearly. Instead, we're encouraged to use more complicated words and sentence structures to show off our learning and literacy. . . . Instead of teaching us how to communicate as clearly as possible, our schooling in English teaches us how to fog things up. It even implants a fear that if we don't make our writing complicated enough, we'll be considered uneducated."

I think everyone can agree that many of the issues we face in life can be complex. A professor may legitimately argue that his or her area of expertise is complicated. I won't contest that. But as leaders and communicators, our job is to bring clarity to a subject, not complexity. It does-n't take nearly as much skill to identify a problem as it does to find a good solution. The measure of a great teacher isn't what he or she knows; it's what the students know. Making things simple is a skill, and it's a necessary one if you want to connect with people when you communicate. Or to put it the way Albert Einstein did, "If you can't explain it simply, you don't understand it enough."

> *The measure of a great teacher isn't what he or she knows; it's what the students know.*

Charlie Wetzel, whom I hired in 1994 to assist me in writing and research, came from an academic background. He has degrees in English, and prior to working with me, he was a teacher and academic dean at a business college. I knew that to do effective research for me, he would have to know what kinds of material I wanted. Stacks of research that wouldn't connect with people would not help me.

I asked other authors what they did to help train someone for such a task, but they were of little help. So Charlie and I devised our own plan. He would read a quote book and mark the items he thought were good, and I would take the same book and do likewise. When we compared our evaluations, we found that what we had selected was 90 percent different! Most of what Charlie picked would be long and pedantic. It reflected his academic background.

He said he was looking for quotes with deep thoughts or insights. I'll tell you the problem with that: what one man sees as a source of insight another man sees as a cure for insomnia. So I gave him criteria for picking good material. For my needs, a quote or illustration had to fit in one or more of these four categories:

- Humor—something that will make people laugh
- Heart—something that will captivate people's emotions
- Hope—something that will inspire people
- Help—something that will assist people in a tangible way

These four things may seem simple, but they are effective.

Armed with that information, Charlie and I tried the process again with another quote book. This time we were in the 50 percent range. And within a few months, Charlie and I agreed on 90 percent of the material he was collecting. Today, fifteen years later, he knows what I want before I do. He practically reads my mind. He writes in my style. He knows my intentions, idiosyncrasies, and passions. He takes my material and makes it better. He rewrites my writing and improves what I want to say. Most importantly, we work hard at keeping things simple.

> *"To be simple is to be great."*
> —RALPH WALDO EMERSON

Being simple is hard work. Mathematician Blaise Pascal once wrote, "I have made this letter longer than usual because I lack the time to make it short." It takes great effort to make any kind of communication concise, precise, and impacting. Or to put it as philosopher-poet Ralph Waldo Emerson did, "To be simple is to be great."

Great communicators leave their audiences with great clarity. Bad ones more often than not leave them confused.

COMMUNICATING ACROSS CULTURES

Keeping communication simple isn't easy. At no time has that been more evident to me than when I try to communicate to audiences and with individuals when I travel internationally. Cross-cultural connecting requires a lot of mental, physical, and emotional energy. And it can sometimes lead to comical results. Here are some interesting signs in English that have been observed in various parts of the world:

- Dry cleaners in Bangkok: *Drop Your Trousers Here for Best Results.*

- Hotel brochure in Italy: *This Hotel Is Renowned for Its Peace and Solitude. In Fact, Crowds from All Over the World Flock Here to Enjoy Its Solitude.*

- In a Tokyo hotel: *Is Forbitten to Steal Hotel Towels Please. If You Are Not Person to Do Such Thing Is Please Not to Read Notis.*

- In a Bucharest hotel lobby: *The Lift Is Being Fixed for the Next Day. During That Time We Regret That You Will Be Unbearable.*

- In a hotel in Athens: *Visitors Are Expected to Complain at the Office between the Hours of 9 and 11 a.m. Daily.*

- In a Rome laundry: *Ladies, Leave Your Clothes Here and Spend the Afternoon Having a Good Time.*

- Outside a Hong Kong tailor shop: *Ladies May Have a Fit Upstairs.*

- In a Rhodes tailor shop: *Order Your Summers Suit. Because Is Big Rush We Will Execute Customers in Strict Rotation.*

- In a Copenhagen airline ticket office: *We Take Your Bags and Send Them in All Directions.*

- At a Budapest zoo: *Please Do No Feed the Animals. If You Have Any Suitable Food, Give It to the Guard on Duty.*

- In an Acapulco hotel: *The Manager Has Personally Passed All the Water Served Here.*

- From a brochure of a car rental firm in Tokyo: *When Passenger of Foot Heave in Sight, Tootle the Horn. Trumpet Him Melodiously at First, But If He Still Obstacles Your Passage Then Tootle Him with Vigor.*[3]

Trust me, if you haven't traveled much internationally, I can tell you that it can be a challenge. After speaking in more than fifty different countries in hundreds of venues, I have developed a "3 S" strategy:

> Keep it **S**imple.
> Say it **S**lowly.
> Have a **S**mile.

If the first two don't work, I hope the third one will at least communicate to people that I like them.

THE ART OF SIMPLICITY

I trust that you will not be disappointed by this chapter because there's not a lot to say about keeping things simple. It's truly a simple concept. However, it's not always easy to do, is it? To help you, I have included five guidelines:

1. TALK TO PEOPLE, NOT ABOVE THEM

A preschool-aged boy was eating an apple in the backseat of the car. "Daddy," he said, "why is my apple turning brown?"

The boy's father explained, "Because after you ate the skin off, the meat of the apple came in contact with the air, which caused it to oxidize, thus changing its molecular structure and turning it into a different color."

There was a long silence, and then the boy asked, "Daddy, are you talking to me?"

A lot of people feel that way when a speaker or leader conveys complex ideas without making the effort to make them clear and simple. I know I've sometimes felt that way as a listener. When this occurs, it means the communicator doesn't understand that shooting above people's heads doesn't mean you have superior ammunition—it means you're a lousy shot.

My first college degree was in theology. While studying for that degree, I was neither taught nor encouraged to speak to an audience in simple terms. In my senior year, I was awarded first prize in a speech contest. My subject wasn't especially audience friendly, and neither was the style of my delivery. I spoke in long sentences and used many big words. My professors were impressed. And so was I . . . until I took my first pastorate in a rural community in southern Indiana. I soon realized that parsing Greek verbs and delving into complex theology was not of great interest to anyone in the congregation.

The people I spoke to on a weekly basis were like the man listening to a U.S. Navy ordnance officer explaining in great detail how guided missiles work. After the talk, the man congratulated the officer on his brilliant presentation, saying, "Before hearing the lecture I was thoroughly confused about how these missiles work."

"And now?" the officer asked.

"Thanks to you," the man replied, "I'm still just as confused, but on a much deeper level."

Once I realized that my "brilliant" talks weren't helping anybody, I started working to change my style. It took effort, but as I've mentioned, I went from being a speaker who wanted to impress others to one who wanted to impact them. The main change came in going from complicated to simple. As my sentences got smaller, my congregation got larger. In time, I realized that one of the greatest compliments I could receive was, "Pastor, I understood everything you said, and it made sense."

The direct and simple approach is usually best in all forms of communication. Janet George wrote to me that after accepting a different position at work, she began training the lady who would take over her old job.

"I showed her the form I had created for communicating with the field offices," says Janet.

"It sounds like it was written on an elementary reading level," the lady commented in a contemptuous tone. "I will be rewriting it to a more adult-sounding communication."

Janet didn't see her for many months, but when she did, the lady confided that her new form had been too hard for the field to understand and she had gone back to the old form.[4]

Greater complexity is never the answer in communication—if your desire is to connect.

2. GET TO THE POINT

A woman getting ready to leave a doctor's office gave the physician a quizzical glance. "Is something the matter?" asked the doctor.

"I'm not sure," answered the woman. "I arrived five minutes early for my appointment. You took me right away. You spent a lot of time with me. I understood every word of your instructions. I can even read your prescription. Are you a real doctor?"

In certain situations, you don't expect others to be clear, concise, and quick. In others you do. Anytime you're getting ready to hear someone speak, if it takes him a long time to get to the point, you know you're in trouble.

Winston Churchill once said about a colleague, "He is one of those orators who, before he gets up, does not know what he is going to say; when he is speaking, does not know what he is saying; and when he has sat down, doesn't know what he has said." What an indictment. I've listened to a few communicators like that. Haven't you? Sadly, I have also been one of them!

All good communicators get to the point before their listeners start asking, "What's the point?" To do that, one must start out already knowing what the point is. Greek playwright Euripides observed, "A bad beginning makes a bad ending." Obviously, the time to start thinking about the reason for your communication is before you begin to speak.

> *All good communicators get to the point before their listeners start asking, "What's the point?"*

Whenever I am preparing to communicate with others, whether to an audience of hundreds or with a single person, I ask myself two questions: "What do I want them to know?" and "What do I want them to do?" If I have clear answers to these two questions, then I am much more likely to stay on track, get to the point, and connect with my listeners.

Perhaps one of the most difficult scenarios for communication is when you have to confront another person. Because of the leadership responsibilities I've had in my career, I have often needed to confront people. Early on, I was insecure and intimidated by such encounters. Too often my strategy was to either talk about a lot of other things first before sharing the bad news, or I'd hint at the problem instead of stating it clearly. It took me many years to take a more direct approach and say what I needed to as quickly as possible.

Tom Arington, the founder and CEO of Prasco Pharmaceutical Company, and I had dinner last year in Cincinnati. We talked about a lot of interesting things that night, including the tough calls that leaders must often make. During our discussion, he shared with me one of his strategies for confronting an employee who isn't being successful. He said, "When I have someone in my company who is not doing well, I ask them two questions: first I ask, 'Do you want to keep your job?' That lets them know there is a problem. Second, 'Do you want me to help you?' That lets them know I am willing to help them." Now, that's getting straight to the point.

Honestly, I think most people would rather others get to the point with them. They prefer the direct approach, especially in a difficult situation. And that reminds me of a humorous story about an employee who found himself in a tight spot. His name was Sam. Everybody except him at the small company where he worked had signed up for a new pension plan in which employees would be required to contribute a small amount every pay period, but the company would pay all other amounts and fees. There was just one catch: the plan would be implemented only if there was 100 percent employee participation.

People tried everything to convince Sam to sign up. His fellow workers alternately pleaded with him and chided him. His boss tried to persuade him, but Sam wouldn't budge. He didn't want to reduce his paycheck by a single cent.

Finally the company president called Sam to his office and said, "Sam, here's a copy of the new pension plan, and here's a pen. You can sign the papers, or you can start looking for a new job because you're fired."

Sam signed the papers without hesitation.

"Now," said the president, "why couldn't you have signed them before?"

"Well, sir," replied Sam, "nobody explained it to me before quite so clearly."

Everyone likes clarity. Even people who are not bottom-line thinkers want to know the bottom line. Good communicators give it to them. Of course, there are times when people communicate in such a way that they purposely obscure their meaning. Nowhere does that seem to happen more than when supervisors are asked for a recommendation by a bad employee. When the person asking for the recommendation isn't someone they want to endorse, their responses can be very creative. Here are a few, along with their "real" meanings, selected for the book, *Lexicon of Intentionally Ambiguous Recommendations (L.I.A.R.)* by Robert Thornton:

RECOMMENDATION	MEANING
She was always high in my opinion.	She was often seen smoking a joint.
While he worked with us he was given numerous citations.	He was arrested many times.
I would say that his real talent is getting wasted at his current job.	He gets bombed regularly.

I am pleased to say that this candidate is a former colleague of mine.	I can't tell you how happy I am that he left our firm.
You simply won't believe this woman's credentials.	She faked most of her résumé.
He would always ask if there was anything he could do.	We were always wondering too.
You will never catch him asleep on the job.	He's too crafty to get caught.
He doesn't know the meaning of the word *quit*.	He can't spell it, either.

If you are communicating with others, whether you're speaking to a child, leading a meeting, or giving a speech to a large audience, your goal should be to get to the point as soon as you have established a connection with people and to make as great an impact on others as you can with as few words as possible. Great leaders and speakers do this consistently.

American founders George Washington and Benjamin Franklin were known to possess this quality. Thomas Jefferson, our nation's third president, wrote of them, "I served with General Washington in the legislature of Virginia before the Revolution and during it with Dr. Franklin in Congress. I never heard either of them speak ten minutes at a time, nor in any but the main point which was to decide the question. They laid their shoulders to the great points, knowing that the little ones would follow of themselves." If we do the same, we will garner the respect of others and increase our chances of remaining connected with people when we speak.

---

3. SAY IT OVER AND OVER AND OVER AND OVER AGAIN

Good teachers know that the fundamental law of learning is repetition. Someone once told me that people have to hear something sixteen times before they really believe it. That seems extreme, yet I do know that repetition is essential in communication if you want people to understand and buy into what you're saying. William H. Rastetter, who taught at MIT and Harvard before becoming CEO of IDEC Pharmaceuticals Corporation, asserts, "The first time you say something, it's heard. The second time, it's recognized, and the third time, it's learned." That's much more optimistic, but it still emphasizes the value of repetition.

If you want to be an effective communicator, you have to be willing to keep emphasizing a point. That's also true if you want to be an effective leader. My friend and founding pastor of Willow Creek church, Bill Hybels, says, "Vision leaks!" By that, he means that even if people do buy into a vision, they can eventually lose their passion and enthusiasm for it. They can even lose sight of the vision altogether. Because that is true, leaders must continually repeat the values and vision of their organization so that employees (or volunteers in churches and other nonprofits) will know those values and visions, think in terms of them, and live them.

> *"The first time you say something, it's heard. The second time, it's recognized, and the third time, it's learned."*
>
> —WILLIAM H. RASTETTER

Articulating a theme and repeating it often can be very challenging. At the most elementary level, you can follow the advice of instructors at the Dale Carnegie School, who tell classes, "Tell the audience what you are going to say. Say it. Then tell them what you've said." A more sophisticated approach is taken by someone like Andy Stanley, the leader of North Point Community Church, a wonderful communicator, and a good friend. He often crafts a message based on a single point—one big idea. And then everything he communicates informs, illustrates, or illuminates that main point. It's a very creative and effective way of making sure he drives his point home, and his audience really connects with the message.

Jim Blanchard, the chairman of Synovus Financial Corp, hosts a leadership conference each year in Columbus, Georgia. Last year I had the privilege of speaking there alongside Pulitzer Prize–winning writer Tom Freidman, former Speaker of the House Newt Gingrich, and author Daniel Pink. During his talk, Daniel made the following statement: "Three words are essential to connect with others (1) brevity, (2) levity, and (3) repetition. Let me say that again!" He brought down the house. And he also connected because he practiced the very thing he advised—in only twenty words. We should try to do the same.

4. SAY IT CLEARLY

The great Cunard liner *Queen Mary* was originally to have been given a different name. The original intention was to christen the ship *Queen Victoria*. However, when a Cunard official was dispatched to Buckingham Palace to inform George V of the choice, the official wasn't clear in his communication. He told the king that the company had decided to name the imposing new vessel after the "greatest of all English queens."

"Oh," the delighted monarch exclaimed, "my wife will be so pleased!" thinking he meant her. The Cunard official didn't have the courage to correct the king's mistake. So he instead went back to the Cunard offices, explained the situation, and the ship was renamed *Queen Mary*.

A mentor of mine in the 1970s, Charles Blair, used to tell me, "Have an understanding so there won't be a misunderstanding." In other words, you must be able to see something clearly in your mind before you can say it clearly with your mouth. Anytime people cannot articulate an idea well, it's a sure sign that they don't possess a good enough understanding of it. This is probably never more evident than when an insecure or ill-informed person in a position of authority speaks. Jack Welch, the former CEO of General Electric, pointed out, "Insecure managers create complexity. Frightened, nervous managers use thick, convoluted planning books and busy slides filled with everything they've known since childhood."[5]

I once became the leader of an organization and inherited a career navy man as the COO. He had created a massive policy manual prior to my arrival, and it made me think of an observation by David Evans, who criticized the way the military tends to communicate. Evans illustrated it with the following simple statement and the kinds of revisions that are implemented in the armed services:

> *"Have an understanding so there won't be a misunderstanding."*
>
> —CHARLES BLAIR

1st Draft: A word to the wise is sufficient.

2nd Draft: A word to the wise may be sufficient.

3rd Draft: It is believed that a word to the wise may be sufficient.

4th Draft: It is believed by some that a word to the wise may be sufficient under some conditions.

5th Draft: Indications are that it is believed by some that a word to the wise may be sufficient under some conditions, although this may possibly vary under differing circumstances. This conclusion may not be supportable under detailed analysis and should be used only in a general sense with a full realization of the underlying assumptions.

My COO's manual was too thick and complicated. As I looked at it, I wondered how my staff could possibly understand and follow it if I couldn't. I got rid of it.

If you're preparing to communicate with an audience, you would be wise to follow the advice of professional speaker Peter Meyer. He says:

Most speakers put too much into their talk. There is only so much you can cover in an hour and expect learning to occur. We have started to follow a specific model to make sure that we do not break this rule. I call it Jigsaw Management.

As you lay out your ideas, imagine that you are going to ask your audience to assemble a large jigsaw puzzle from scratch. Your ideas are the pieces.

When you are doing a puzzle, the first thing that you do is to look at the boxtop. Your talk should have one of those. It tells you which pieces you want to present.

Now, how many ideas do you have in your puzzle? Remember how much harder it is to assemble a 1000-piece puzzle than a 100-piece one if you only have an hour to do it? If you have more than a few main ideas, you have too many. I keep my talks to three ideas max, and that can still be too much for an hour.

Ask yourself another question before you start organizing your talk. If you were playing with a puzzle and you had only an hour to finish, would you want the person with the puzzle to hide the boxtop from you? Would you want the person to add extra pieces to the pile? Don't be guilty of the same when you do your talks.

In other words, no matter how wonderful the idea is to you, don't include it unless it fits exactly into the picture on your boxtop.

Second, as you start the talk, be sure to tell your audience what the boxtop looks like. Tell them what you will show them so they know where the ideas fit.

In the end, people are persuaded not by what we say, but by what they understand. When you speak clearly and simply, more people can understand what you're trying to communicate. Being simple as a communicator isn't a weakness. It's a strength! Author and critic John Ruskin observed, "The greatest thing a human ever does in the world is to see something

> *In the end, people are persuaded not by what we say, but by what they understand.*

and tell others what he saw in a plain way. Hundreds can talk for one who can think, but thousands can think for one who can see. To see clearly and tell others clearly is poetry, prophecy, and religion all in one."

5. SAY LESS

Recently I was on tap to speak at a program that had been over-scheduled and as a result was running far behind schedule. As the clock ticked away and my time to speak approached, I could see that the host was getting anxious. As I got ready to go onstage, he nervously explained that my slot, which was originally scheduled for an hour, had been reduced to only thirty minutes. I made light of the situation and tried to reassure him by saying, "Don't worry. I'll give my pizza speech. If I don't deliver in less than thirty minutes, you don't have to pay me." I made some adjustments on the fly, and everything turned out fine.

Many people become very protective of their time on the platform or their opportunity to speak in a meeting. They love being onstage, and as far as they're concerned, the more time they have in front of other people, the better they like it. True, I admit that I enjoy communicating with people. It energizes me. And even when I am required to speak all day at a seminar, I walk away excited, not exhausted. However, at the same time, I've also discovered that when I speak for less time and do so more succinctly, people remember it better and longer. Isn't that ironic?

> *"He can compress the most words in the smallest ideas of any man I ever met."*
>
> —ABRAHAM LINCOLN

Take a moment and think about all the teachers, speakers, preachers, politicians, and leaders you've listened to over the years. What percentage of the time have you come away from a session thinking, *I sure wish he had spoken longer; that was just too short?* I'd be willing to bet the percentage is very small. Unfortunately, more than 90 percent of the time, people wear out their welcome when they communicate. They're like the politician about whom Abraham Lincoln said, "He can compress the most words in the smallest ideas of any man I ever met."

Executive communication coach Anne Cooper Ready, in her book *Off the Cuff,* gives the following advice:

Begin, and end, on time. Or better yet, end a little early. Even if you are a paid speaker and want to impress the organizers so they know they've gotten their money's worth, stop yourself with a particularly good answer a few minutes before you have to. In today's over-booked society, nothing is more appreciated than the gift of a little found time.

According to Ronald Reagan's speechwriter, Peggy Noonan, he believed that no one wants to sit in an audience in respectful silence for more than 20 minutes. Then, offer up to 20 minutes of Q&A and everyone gets to go home!

Nothing is worse than keeping an audience trapped into the night. Don't fall in love with the sound of your own words. You will undo all the good you've done by dragging it out to get in just one more point. By finishing a bit early, you leave everything and everyone on a positive note, hopefully wanting more for the next time.[6]

You can hardly go wrong by keeping things short when you communicate. But there are a million ways to go wrong by talking too long.

One of the greatest ovations I ever received came at the end of the shortest speech I've ever given. It was at a banquet following a charity golf event. It had been a very long day. We had all played in the tournament, the program was going way too long, and I could see that the golfers were tired and restless.

Finally after three hours of programming, the emcee shared with the audience that I would be coming up as the keynote speaker to talk to them on the subject of leadership. After what could only be described as polite applause, I stepped up to the podium and said, "It's been a long day and a long program. Most of us are tired. My leadership talk is the following: Everything rises and falls on leadership."

Then I left the podium and sat down.

For a moment there was a stunned silence. Then all of a sudden, the crowd erupted. With great appreciation, everybody rose to give me a standing ovation. I promise you, it is a speech they will never forget!

Now, I don't recommend that you start giving only six-word speeches. (This is the only time in more than forty years of speaking that I did that.) Most of the time you are asked to speak, your host expects more of you. You are expected to add value to your audience, and rarely can you do that with so few words. But anytime you communicate—whether to one person or one hundred—it is always a good idea to try to keep it simple. Nobody gives you extra points for being obscure or difficult.

Winston Churchill was perhaps the greatest communicator of the twentieth century. He was an excellent leader, an inspiring communicator, and an accomplished writer, receiving the Nobel Prize for Literature in 1953. He continually expressed the importance of keeping communication simple. He stated, "All the great things are simple, and many can be expressed in a single word: freedom, justice, honor, duty, mercy, hope," and "Broadly speaking, the short words are the best, and the old words best of all."

It may seem counterintuitive, but if you want to take your communication to the next level and connect with people, don't try to impress them with your intellect or overpower them with too much information. Give them clarity and simplicity. People will relate to you, you will connect, and they'll want to invite you back to communicate with them again.

CONNECTING WITH PEOPLE AT ALL LEVELS

CONNECTING PRACTICE: Connectors do the difficult work of keeping it simple.

KEY CONCEPT: The larger the group, the simpler the communication needs to be.

CONNECTING ONE-ON-ONE

Helping one other person to understand what you have to say is usually fairly easy. Why? Because you can tailor it exactly to his or her personality, experience, and intellect. And if you're not crystal clear in your communication, you will probably be able to read it in the person's expression. You can also answer any questions the person may ask. Of course, that still doesn't mean you can be lazy. If you want to connect, not just get across a bunch of information, you should still work to keep it simple. The more easily understood you are, the better your chances of connecting with your listener.

CONNECTING IN A GROUP

Communicating in a group is a little more complicated than communicating one-on-one. You have to make your ideas work for more than one person, so simplify them. You should never simply "dump" a bunch of information on people and expect them to sort it out. That's lazy and ineffective. If you've been given the opportunity to speak, do the hard work of making communication simple. To make sure you have been effective, do the following:

- Ask for feedback.

- Ask people in the group to share what they have learned.

- Ask the group to tell how they are going to pass what you've said on to others.

CONNECTING WITH AN AUDIENCE

There's a real art to making communication simple but memorable. It took me years to learn how to do it. Two good ways to approach a message are to ask yourself: "What are the bare essentials that I need to communicate for people to understand it?" and "How can I make those few essential points memorable?"

Another trick that good leaders use to sharpen a message for something important, such as the communication of vision, is to practice first by telling a single person. If it works well for an individual, then they try it with a small, hand-selected group. That way the communicator can read people's expressions, see what works, and also receive people's input. (Sometimes when I do this, I'll even ask people to explain what I just said to the person next to them.) Only after an important communication has been tested do speakers then take it to the masses.

8

CONNECTORS CREATE AN EXPERIENCE EVERYONE ENJOYS

What words would you choose to describe the best communicators who have connected well with you? Entertaining? Energetic? Funny? Maybe if you gave it some time, you could produce a long list of attributes. Now think about the people you don't care for, the ones who were unable to connect with you. If I asked you to describe them using only one word, what would it be? I'm willing to bet that the word would be *boring*. That is the one word that best describes someone who doesn't connect with others. Every day, everywhere, millions of eyes glaze over in classrooms, auditoriums, churches, meeting rooms, and living rooms because the people speaking fail to be interesting, and as a result, they don't connect.

How many lessons that you sat through in a classroom do you actually remember? How many conversations? Or speeches? For every one you remember, there have probably been thousands you don't. Corporate presentations coach Jerry Weissman points out, "Few human activities are done as often as presentations, and as poorly. One recent estimate has it that 30 million presentations using Microsoft PowerPoint slides are made every day. I'm sure that you've attended more than a few. How many of them were truly memorable, effective, and persuasive? Probably only a handful."

Well, here's some good news: no matter what your current level of skill is in this area, you can make it better. Being interesting can be learned. I know because my personal experience can back it up. In my early years, I was not an interesting speaker. In fact, before my first job while I was still in college, I took a test that measured creativity. My score was at the bottom of my class! I thought, *Oh no, I'm going to be another boring preacher.*

That's when I started the discipline of collecting quotes, stories, and illustrations for my speaking. I figured if *I* couldn't be interesting, at the very least I would include things in my messages that were.

Of course, no matter how hard you work at connecting with people and try to be interesting, you can't please everyone. My children were young when I was a full-time pastor preaching nearly every Sunday. On Saturday nights when I would pray with my daughter Elizabeth, she would often pray, "Dear God, please help Daddy not to be boring tomorrow." I also overheard her telling her younger brother, Joel, one Sunday morning to take a lot of stuff to church with him because I was preaching.

What can I say? I often identified with the pastor who was asked by his daughter why he always prayed before he entered the pulpit.

"Honey," he answered, "I do that to ask God to help me with my sermon."

The little girl thought for a minute and replied, "Then why doesn't he, Daddy?"

I can hardly blame my children. As a kid growing up in church, my prayer on Sunday morning went something like this . . .

Now I lay me down to sleep,
The sermon's long; the subject's deep.
If he should quit before I wake,
I ask someone, "Give me a shake."

My brother, sister, and I often felt the way my children did—we were bored. Too often the preachers we heard did exactly what Ronald Reagan's most prominent speechwriter, Peggy Noonan, advised against. They gave what she called the hammock speech: "The speech that has a nice strong tree holding it at one end, at the beginning, and a nice strong tree holding it up at the other end, at the coda, and in the middle there is this nice soft section where we all fall asleep." You can't do that if you want to maintain a positive connection with your audience!

HOW TO BE INTERESTING

After giving thousands of speeches and communicating for decades, I have learned some things about how to be interesting to others and make communication an experience everyone enjoys. I'm going to present to you the best of the best of what I've learned—when I'm working with one person, leading a group, and speaking to audiences. As you prepare to communicate, no matter whether it's to one, one hundred, or one thousand, try to do as many of these seven things as possible:

1. TAKE RESPONSIBILITY FOR YOUR LISTENERS

I often hear presenters talk about bad audiences they've spoken to. Usually they are describing people who don't respond favorably to their speeches. I think they've got it wrong. In general, there are no bad audiences; only bad speakers. If the audience is asleep, somebody needs to go onstage and wake up the speaker!

> *In general, there are no bad audiences; only bad speakers.*

Brent Filson's book *Executive Speeches* contains advice on speaking from fifty-one CEOs. One executive wrote, "The Constitution guarantees free speech, but it doesn't guarantee listeners. Even if you do get listeners, there is no guarantee that they will be listening. So your first responsibility as a speaker is to gain and keep the audience's attention. Whatever your purpose, you have the best chance for success when you know that their attention is your responsibility, yours alone." Great communicators take responsibility for others' responses to them, even in tough settings under difficult conditions.

Almost everyone has heard the expression, "You can lead a horse to water, but you can't make him drink." That may be true. But it's also true that you can feed a horse salt and make him thirsty. In other words, you can work to keep your listeners engaged.

When I am speaking to people, I feel it is my responsibility to make it an enjoyable learning experience. *How can I capture their attention? What is necessary to make this speech memorable? How can I capture their attention and keep them with me to the very end?*

Too often people step up in front of people with the expectation that it's the listener's responsibility to "get" what the speaker is talking about and to respond to it favorably. They have a take-it-or-leave-it mind-set. What a mistake. I call that cemetery communication: lots

of people are out there, but nobody is listening. To avoid becoming that kind of speaker, I take responsibility when I communicate. I never forget that it's my job to create interest in listeners, activate the audience, enjoy the experience, and add value to others. When I can do that, my mission has been accomplished. I have connected.

I've tried to maintain that same mind-set when writing books. When I began writing, I often felt inadequate in keeping the interest of the reader. One-on-one, I'm a pretty good conversationalist. And as a speaker, I had learned to use charisma to engage the audience. I showed a genuine interest in people. I used positive body language, facial expressions, and tone of

> *Cemetery communication: lots of people are out there, but nobody is listening.*

voice to keep people's interest. I had fun, and the audience often had fun with me. As a writer, I didn't possess that advantage any longer. I often wondered how I could make my books interesting. What helped me was something I read about historian Barbara Tuchman. During all the years she wrote, she had a little sign over her typewriter that said, "Will the reader turn the page?" She didn't take for granted her reader's response; she took responsibility for it.

For years as I have sat with a legal pad to write, I have asked myself that same question. It reminds me to take responsibility for the reader's interest. As I begin writing, I think, *What would make me want to read about this?* After I have written a chapter, I try to read it from the perspective of people who might pick the book up. *What will motivate them to turn the page? What will encourage them to finish the book?*

I also take responsibility for creating an experience that others will enjoy when I'm with a small group of people. If we're having dinner, I work to create good conversation. I think, *What can I say to get others involved around the table? How can I draw them in?* If I take friends on a trip or out for a night on the town, I try to create memories. For example, several years ago I invited Dan and Patti Reiland and Tim and Pam Elmore to join Margaret and me for a weekend in New York City. One night we ate dinner at Tavern on the Green, a restaurant in Central Park that is a major tourist destination. Afterward, we wanted to go to Macy's, and instead of walking or taking a cab, we hired three bicycle-powered rickshaws, one for each couple. To make it memorable, I told the three drivers that it was a race, and whoever got to Macy's first would get an additional fifty-dollar tip.

Well, you can imagine what happened. We all got whiplash as the drivers took off. They weaved in and out of traffic. They cut in front of one another. A couple of times I thought we were going to tip over. It was the most exciting two-mile trip we'd ever taken. It was and is a great memory.

You may think that giving a driver a fifty-dollar tip was extravagant. Maybe it was. But what price do you put on a great memory? It connected us! And it's something all of us will remember until the day we die. I'd say that was worth the price—and worth the effort. As a leader, I believe it's a privilege and a responsibility to give people experiences they enjoy. As a husband, father, and now grandfather, it's even more important to me. Creating positive, memorable experiences does more to connect families than just about anything else. I strongly encourage you to take responsibility for it.

2. COMMUNICATE IN THEIR WORLD

When I was a kid growing up, fathers generally didn't share parenting duties the way most do today. Men and women often lived in different worlds. Back in those days of cloth diapers, a man whose obsession was baseball was out for dinner with his wife when their baby started to cry. The lady had spent the entire day taking care of the child, and she was exhausted. So she asked her husband to change his son's diaper.

"I don't know how to change a baby," said the husband, trying to get out of the job.

"Look, buster," she said, giving him a withering look, "you lay the diaper out like a diamond. You put second base on home plate. Put the baby's bottom on the pitcher's mound, hook up first and third, and slide home underneath. And if it starts to rain, the game ain't called—you start all over again."

If you want to get your message across, you have to learn how to communicate in someone else's world. Connecting with others requires this skill. Too often speakers are unwilling or unable to get out of their own world and say things from the perspective of their listeners. When that happens, not only is it unlikely that a connection will develop; it actually creates distance between speaker and listener.

Engineering senior manager Lars Ray commented,

I am often required to present ideas or solutions to new products being developed. Unless I am speaking to other engineers who eat this stuff for breakfast, this is dry, boring material. Since there are always people from the management, leadership, or finance teams present in the audience, I have to take the responsibility for them as well and ensure that what is communicated reaches all participants in a way that is meaningful and actionable . . . rather than assuming they understand engineering speak.[1]

One of my early communication challenges occurred because I thought the people who listened to me were as interested in my sub-

> *People don't remember what we think is important; they remember what they think is important.*

ject as I was. All week long I would work to prepare a message for Sunday. I thought my congregation would approach Sunday with the same anticipation I would. But the reality was that they were living their lives—working, spending time with family, running errands, playing sports, visiting with friends, and so on. Nobody was waiting with bated breath to hear me speak. And when Sunday rolled around, I couldn't expect them to enter my world. If I wanted to connect, I had to meet them in *their* world.

The same thing is true for people in the business world, especially for salespeople and others who work with customers or clients. Speaker, trainer, and author Teri Sjodin says:

> On average, prospects retain only half of what we tell them. Before an hour has passed, they lose 10 percent of the little they originally knew. After sleeping on it, guess what? Another 20 percent evaporates. By the time the breakfast rush has subsided, they have avoided two near-collisions on the freeway, found notes on their desk from their bosses, and they have forgotten another 10 percent. So the entire time we have assumed a prospect has been thinking about our proposal, he or she has been forgetting about it.

To connect with others in their world, you can't just live in your own world. You have to link what you want to say to what others' needs are. People don't remember what *we* think is important; they remember what *they* think is important. That's why it's a good idea whenever possible to avoid using abstract terms and make what you say personal. If you're part of the leadership team of an organization, don't talk about what "management" believes or what "leadership" intends to implement. Say what you are doing. If you're speaking to employees, don't talk about them as though they weren't there; address them directly. Better yet, whenever you can say it with credibility, use "we" to include your listeners when talking about *everyone* on the team. It goes back to the old saying:

> Talk at me and you'll talk alone.
> Talk to me and I'll listen.
> Talk about me and I'll listen for hours.

Anything you can do to relate to your listeners and meet them on *their* terms is going to help you connect—as long as you maintain authenticity. You can't pretend to be someone you're not. You have to be yourself while speaking someone else's language.

3. Capture People's Attention from the Start

Management consultant Myrna Marofsky quipped, "People have remote controls in their heads today. If you don't catch their interest, they just click you off." Haven't you found that people can "check out" very quickly when you start talking? I have. As a speaker, I've discovered that I don't have much time before people either tune in or turn off. And if they turn off, I have to work very hard to try to win them back—if I can at all. That's why I do everything in my power to make a good first impression and start well when I communicate.

> *"People have remote controls in their heads today. If you don't catch their interest, they just click you off."*
>
> —MYRNA MAROFSKY

People make quick judgments about us all the time, not just when we're communicating to a group. As Sonya Hamlin suggests, from the moment when others first meet us, they are consciously or unconsciously evaluating us and deciding whether to keep listening or simply dismiss us. She says, "If we're not captured by something in those first moments, it's, 'Excuse me, I see a friend,' and off they go."

Most of the time, we have an instantaneous reaction to people, and we are either drawn to them or not. I know that's true for me. When people smile, make eye contact, and try to initiate contact in some way, by saying hello or reaching out to shake my hand, it puts me in a much more positive frame of mind toward them.

When I speak to an audience, I try to initiate in a positive way, just as I do one-on-one. More specifically, here are some of the things I do:

Start with a Comment About the Situation or Setting. Before experienced communicators speak, they pay attention to what's going on around them. They are aware of what's been happening. They try to know who has been speaking and what has happened in the audience. They pay attention to any comments that have been made. Then when they get up to speak, they use that to their advantage. The next time you speak, say something based on what everyone has just experienced. That puts you on the same page with your listeners and helps them feel connected to you.

Introduce Yourself. Often when I speak, one of the first things I do is simply say, "Hi, my name is John. What's your name?" When most of the individuals in the audience shout out names at me, it creates a bit of energetic chaos. Then we all get a good laugh out of it. That may sound corny, but it breaks the ice, and people start to feel connected with me.

Relax. In a previous chapter I mentioned that I discovered I could be much more relaxed in front of an audience when I sat on a stool. It lets people know that I am comfortable and want them to feel that way also. My posture is that of someone who wants to converse *with* them, not talk *at* them. When I'm at ease and enjoy the experience, the people are more likely to enjoy it too. If you can find a way to show your listeners that you are relaxed but attentive to them, you can usually put them at ease.

Begin with Humor. Once when I was the keynote speaker at a banquet that seemed to go on forever, when I finally got up to speak, I opened with the following story: "At 8,578 words, President William Henry Harrison's inaugural address was the longest ever. He read it on a cold, raw inaugural day, refusing to wear either hat or coat. The cold he caught that day turned into pneumonia. He died one month later."

Then I said, "As a speaker, I have learned a lesson from this bit of history. I will remain dressed, and I promise you, my speech will be short." The room erupted with laughter, everyone realized I was going to make my session fun, and we connected.

Create a Sense of Anticipation. At the beginning of many speaking sessions, I share with people that I'm going to add value to their lives. And often I'll say, "You are about to learn something," and then I ask them to tell that to the person beside them. As people turn to one another, the energy in the room increases and anticipation begins to rise. And when I ask them to say to that other person, "And it's about time," they laugh, and many of them actually do say it. It's usually fun for most people, and afterward they feel more connected to me and each other.

Certainly I don't recommend that you do everything that I do. What works for me may not work for you. As you communicate, you need to find your own style and experiment with techniques that suit you. But the principle is still the same. You need to find ways to connect with your listeners early, put them at ease, and get them interested from the start. Find ways to make the experience enjoyable.

4. ACTIVATE YOUR AUDIENCE

It's easy to communicate with people who are highly energetic and active. It's much more difficult with people who are passive. What should you do in such situations? Should you just move forward and hope for the best? Of course not. You should work to activate your audience and get them involved.

Whenever I speak, I look for signs of involvement from the people I'm communicating with. I check to see if they are taking notes. I look to see if people are displaying a "listener's lean." Are people making eye contact? Are they nodding with approval or understanding? Am I getting an audible response from some of the things I say? Are people laughing or applauding? If there are signs of life, great! If there aren't, then I get to work trying to get audience members involved. Here's how:

Ask Questions. Whether you are communicating one-on-one or with a large audience, asking questions creates a connection between you and your listeners that is vital to releasing energy and raising their interest levels. Because my audiences are often so varied, when I begin speaking I sometimes ask what states people are from, and I'll make jokes about the various places. Or I'll pose a question related to the topic I'll be speaking on. I'm simply trying to get people to engage right away.

As I continue speaking, I often ask more broad and inclusive questions. They're usually questions that 90 percent of the people will respond to. For example, if I'm speaking on the subject of failure, I'll ask questions such as "How many of you have made a mistake at least one time in your life?" That usually gets a mild laugh,

and people raise their hands. Most people want to feel a part of the experience, yet they don't want to stand out in a group. If you ask questions that are too specific, people won't raise their hands.

I recommend that you try it, but always start with a big win—a question that will get a lot of response, even a laugh of recognition. Then keep the ball rolling by asking one more. Once they get the idea, they'll like doing it.

I use questions in much less formal settings as well. Before I go to dinner with people, I think of a couple of questions I will ask them such as, "What exciting things have happened to you this month?" or "What good books have you read lately?" I don't wait for people to get involved. I do things that invite them into the process.

Get People Moving. When I speak to an audience, it's often for an entire morning or afternoon. Sometimes after people have been sitting for a long time, I ask them to stand and stretch. Every thirty minutes or so, most people need some type of physical action. Movement gives everyone a quick break from the routine.

Sometimes I will ask people to do an exercise in their seats. For example, when I teach about how difficult change can be or about how it feels different when we try to do something new, I'll ask them to clasp both of their hands together with the fingers intertwined. Invariably, people are used to doing this with a particular thumb on top. So I ask them to clasp their hands again, but this time to do it with the opposite thumb on top. This always gets a reaction because it feels odd. The result is that energy in the room goes up.

Getting people moving also works in groups and one-on-one. You can plan activities for a group that will help them to get energized. And if communication is getting stale when you're meeting with a single person, you can go for a walk or change where you're sitting. Physical activity can help create mental activity.

Ask People to Interact. Though this doesn't work in every setting, I sometimes ask people to interact with one another. Sometimes I ask people to introduce themselves to others around them. Or I'll ask people to share an idea with someone sitting beside them. Or I'll put people into discussion groups.

Once again, this requires people to become involved, and it usually increases the energy in the room. The main point is that it's the speaker's responsibility to bring energy to the audience and to work to activate them.

5. SAY IT SO IT STICKS

All great communication has one thing in common: the speaker said something that people remembered long after the talk was finished. Here are a few examples:

- Patrick Henry—"Give me liberty or give me death."

- Nathan Hale—"I regret that I have but one life to give for my country."

- Abraham Lincoln—"A government of the people, by the people, for the people."

- Winston Churchill—"Never, never, never give up."

- John F. Kennedy—"Ask not what your country can do for you. Ask what you can do for your country."

- Martin Luther King Jr.—"I have a dream."

- Ronald Reagan—"Mr. Gorbachev, tear down this wall."

If you want people to remember what you say, you need to say the right thing at the right moment in the right way!

Early in my career, I often just said what I thought and didn't give enough attention to how I said it. As I came to realize the importance of how something is worded, I worked at it more, but to be honest, my early efforts were a little bit clunky. I've continued working on this skill, and over the years, I have learned to say things in ways that people will remember. I want to share with you some of the things I've learned:

> *If you want people to remember what you say, you need to say the right thing at the right moment in the right way!*

Link What You Say with What People Need. Nothing makes a speech more memorable than need. When Churchill said, "Never, never, never give up," people were facing the threat of the Nazis conquering all of Europe. When Martin Luther King Jr. told people at the Lincoln Memorial that he had a dream, they needed his inspiration to keep fighting for civil rights.

People pay attention when something that is said connects with something they greatly desire. If you follow my advice about trying to communicate with people on common ground and you make an effort to enter their world when you speak, then you increase your chances of understanding their needs and wants. And that increases your ability to connect.

Find a Way to Be Original. Studies have shown that there's a direct correlation between predictability and impact. The more predictable listeners think you are, the lower the impact you make on them. Conversely, if you lower your predictability, you increase your impact. If your audience always knows what's coming, they'll check out.

Production manager Joseph Marler says he fights predictability by doing a magic trick in business settings.[2] Pastor Robert Keen told me

> *People pay attention when something that is said connects with something they greatly desire.*

that he once put a vase in a plastic bag and smashed it with a hammer to get people's attention—but he hit it so hard that glass flew everywhere. Robert says, "The congregation was in hysterical laughter as I tried to gather myself."[3] And Jeff Roberts explained that he took a boring senior project presentation for his degree in entrepreneurship and converted it into a rhyming Dr. Seuss-inspired presentation complete with a poster board storybook. It got a standing ovation. "Our professor, who was known for his strict grading," says Jeff, "gave us a 100%, which had previously been unheard of. He said he had never experienced any presentation like it and had never seen students listen so intently and be as captivated as our audience was . . . By creating an experience that everyone enjoyed, we were able to elevate the typical class presentation, engage the audience, and make it a day of fun and laughter for a group of hardworking students coming to the end of their college career."[4]

Use Humor. Proverbs says, "A cheerful heart is good medicine."[5] Even when audience members have a tough time remembering some of the points you make, they often recall the humor you use. After all, everyone loves humor, especially self-deprecating humor. It shows the humanness of the presenter. Anytime someone makes light of himself, it connects him with people rather than putting him above them. President Abraham Lincoln, who was known as the people's president, often poked fun at himself. And history honors him for this human quality. It's a technique that every communicator should embrace.

Use a Shocking Statement or Statistic. I will never forget what Nancy Beach said in a message regarding poverty: "Six million children under the age of five die every year as a result of starvation. One in seven people in the world go to bed hungry every day. The three richest people in the world have more wealth collectively than the combined Gross National Product of the world's forty-eight poorest countries."[6]

Don't you find those numbers surprising? I did. And that's why they stayed with me. If you have information on your topic that will grab people's attention, then use it.

Of course, you can also use statistics humorously to connect with people. Duke Brekhus says, "One of my favorite anonymous quotes regarding statistics is that 37.5 percent of all statistics are made up on the spot! It always gets a laugh!"[7]

Say Things in an Interesting Way. If you simply give people information or communicate ideas with no thought to the phrasing you use, you're missing opportunities to connect and for people to remember what you say. Compare these phrases:

A person must sacrifice to get to the top.	You have to give up to go up.
Relationships are important to influence people.	People won't go along with you if they can't get along with you.
People won't listen until they know that you care.	People don't care how much you know until they know how much you care.

Anytime you can say something in a fresh or clever way, people are more likely to pay attention.

Learn to Pause. Connecting with people is a two-way street. It is a dialogue, not a monologue. Anytime you engage in nonstop speaking without pausing, people's minds will disengage. However, if you pause, even for a moment, you give people a chance to consider

> *Connecting with people is a two-way street. It is a dialogue, not a monologue.*

what you've just said. It gives their minds a needed break. And the best time to do this is when you're saying something especially significant.

Many people are insecure with silence. I have made it my friend. When I am communicating and I pause, I am conveying these thoughts: "This is important . . . think about this . . . consider this in the context of what has been said . . . underline it in your mind." I value pauses because they allow people to catch up with a worthwhile statement. My advice to anyone who wants to connect with others is to get comfortable with silence and learn to let it become an exclamation point for things you say.

6. BE VISUAL

Most people learn visually. And in our current age of television, movies, YouTube, and other forms of visual communication, what people see has become increasingly important. There was a time when groups of people would sit around a radio and listen for news and entertainment, but those days are gone.

One of the books that had a strong impact on my communication when I was a pastor was *The Empowered Communicator* by Calvin Miller. In it he wrote a series of letters from imagined audience members to speakers. In one of them he wrote:

Dear Speaker:

The world has never gotten over its likin' of the truth. I've been a member of a church now for more'n fifty years. We must have had twenty pastors or more. I don't know for sure. None of 'em stayed very long. Every one of them told the truth. In fact they could bore you for hours on end with the truth. There was only one out of the whole bunch that we ever really wanted to keep. He told the truth interestingly. One time he put on his bathrobe and played like he was King David. Sure was interesting. Another time he played like he was the innkeeper in Bethlehem. Then one time he smeared his face with soot—sure looked strange—and told us he was Job. We all knew better and he knew we did, but I never really understood the Book of Job till that sermon. One time he dressed up in a white robe and came in the back of the auditorium carrying a sign. He told us he was an Archangel. He seemed so convinced, we believed him. Darndest thing, he'd do per't near't anything to keep our attention. He always did. Big church down in Chattanooga hire him away from us. The good 'uns always seem to get away.

They arrested a man over by Greenville the other day. They threw him in jail. He was walking around town in a white robe, carrying a sign that said "THE WORLD IS COMING TO AN END." I don't know why they arrested him. Most everybody believed he was right. As I saw it, he was telling the truth interestingly. Last week my preacher preached on that very thing. The way he told that same truth wasn't all that interesting. They might have locked up the wrong man.

It sure seems important to me to tell the truth interestingly. Not too many people do it. A bunch of us who listen to your sermons are wishing you'd do it. You might try the white robe and sign routine. Just don't go outside.

—Your Audience

Not everyone can pull off the communication style Miller describes in this letter, but that's not the point. What's important is that as communicators, we need to find a way to appeal visually to our listeners in some way. Some presenters use film or PowerPoint or graphics. None of those things works especially well for me. Instead when I speak, I often use movement and facial expressions. I also use eye contact. All of these things help me to connect visually, though having good eye contact isn't always a sign of great connection. Candace Sargent wrote to tell me about a speaker who saw a woman in the audience who sustained intense direct eye contact with him the whole time he spoke. "It thrilled him," said Candace, "and boosted his confidence even higher! Afterward, he found out she was deaf and just needed to read his lips."[8]

Anything that can help people visually helps them to connect. I encourage people to take notes. When you've written something down, it is more likely to stay with you. Once at a conference, my friends Terry and Jen Brown gave me a T-shirt that I love to wear. It says, "If I'm talking, you should be taking notes." Isn't that the way many people feel when they teach or speak?

I also use words to try to stimulate the imagination of my listeners. I want to encourage them to paint vivid pictures in their minds. When I first began sharing my vision for recruiting and training one million leaders worldwide with my organization, EQUIP, I used the word *imagine* often when I communicated. I would ask people to imagine what would happen to developing countries if leaders were trained to lead, or I'd say, "Imagine how you would feel if you invested your time and money in equipping leaders to make a difference in their world." People began to create their own visuals, they engaged, and they stayed interested.

7. TELL STORIES

Perhaps the most effective way to capture people's interest and make the experience enjoyable when you talk is to include stories. Whether you are communicating humor, hard facts, or tragedy, storytelling improves the experience. Isak Dinesen, quoting a friend, remarked, "All sorrows can be borne if you put them into a story or tell a story about them." Cold facts rarely connect with people. But good stories have an incredible impact and can help even the weakest communicator improve and begin to connect with people.

Though I understood this in conversations and as a speaker, it was a more difficult lesson for me to learn when it came to writing books. I am a bottom-line person. My attitude is usually: *just give me the principles, and I will apply them to my life.* As a result, my first several books lacked the warmth of my public speaking. Honestly, I wrote books for people like me. They were what I would want to read. They were simple, practical, and applicable. They were filled with lists and great quotes I had collected. But they lacked warmth.

A friend really helped me understand what I was doing wrong when he pointed out, "When you speak, you share interesting stories with your audience. You take people on a journey with you. That's what needs to happen in your books." He was right. People connect with stories, not statistics. And that's when I started including more stories in my books.

All great communicators use stories. Abraham Lincoln, perhaps the United States' greatest president, remarked, "They say I tell a great many stories; I reckon I do, but I have found in the course of a long experience that common people, take them as they run, are more easily informed through the medium of a broad illustration than in any other way, and as to what the hypercritical few may think, I don't care."

Neurologists say that our brains are programmed much more for stories than for abstract ideas or PowerPoint slides. Stories, after all, are as old as the human race. We live them, and we love to tell them. We use stories to make sense of our experience. And when we share them, we help people understand us, themselves, and their world.

I love how the impact of storytelling is described in Eugene Peterson's *The Message*. When the disciples asked Jesus why he told so many stories, he replied,

> You've been given insight into God's kingdom. You know how it works. Not everybody has this gift, this insight; it hasn't been given to them. Whenever someone has a ready heart for this, the insights and understandings flow freely. But if there is no readiness, any trace of receptivity soon disappears. That's why I tell stories: to create readiness, to nudge the people toward receptive insight. In their present state they can stare till doomsday and not see it, listen till they're blue in the face and not get it. (Matt. 13:10–13)

For years I have built the reputation of a communicator who draws people into my talks. One of my secrets is that I collect great stories and use them when I speak. I have a collection of laminated cards that contain the best stories I've ever found. When I pull out one of these cards in front of people who have heard me speak before, they can be sure of four things: I will read them the card. It will be humorous. It will teach a point. And I will read it to them as if it is the first time I have ever read it. I believe there is a humanness about sitting on a stool, pulling out a card, and sharing its contents. If you memorize pieces like that and deliver them to a group of people, it can come across as slick and actually create a gap between you and them. However, reading them, if done correctly, can close that gap and help you connect. I've found it to be an enjoyable experience for me and for my listeners.

BE THE COMMUNICATOR YOU WANT TO HEAR

The bottom line when it comes to holding people's interest and connecting with others is that you should try to be the kind of communicator *you* would like to hear. Which communicators do you enjoy listening to? Who connects with you when they speak? What qualities have you observed in the people you admire as communicators?

Sonya Hamlin, in her book *How to Talk So People Listen*, gets to the heart of the matter when she presents two lists of qualities found in many communicators and asks her readers to pick which list best represents the kind of speaker they would like to see. Here are her lists:

LIST 1	LIST 2
Warm	Pompous
Honest	Vague
Friendly	Flat
Exciting	Complex
Interesting	Patronizing
Knowledgeable	Nervous
Organized	Formal
Creative	Irrelevant
Confident	Stuffy
Inspiring	Monotonous
Open	Intense
Authentic	Closed
Informal	
Funny	

Hamlin goes on to describe how the qualities from each of the lists impact us positively and negatively. But I think it's easy to see why the first set of qualities would work well with us and the second wouldn't. The next time you hear someone communicate, I think it would be a good exercise to take these two lists. As you notice one of the qualities, make a check mark next to it. When you come across a communicator whose style and qualities are reflected in LIST 1, study the person to see if there are techniques he or she uses in order to be interesting that you might be able to adopt as well.

No one can connect with everybody. It doesn't matter how hard you work at it. Though I strive to be an effective communicator, I know there are people I leave cold when I talk. That's okay. But you can be sure that I will do everything in my power to keep them from falling asleep. The longer they stay engaged, the better the chance I have of winning them over. And the better the chance of adding value to them.

BE THE PERSON WITH WHOM YOU WANT TO CONNECT

One of my concerns about this chapter was that it puts a lot of emphasis on public speaking—perhaps too much. There are a lot of public speakers who don't connect, and there are a lot of connectors who don't speak publicly. I've tried to provide some tools for people who desire to improve their speaking, but I want to remind you that connecting isn't primarily about learning to become a better presenter. It's about becoming the kind of person others want to connect with.

Billy Hawkins wrote and told me a story that beautifully illustrates what it means to connect by creating an experience that someone enjoys. She explained:

We had a young six-year-old boy, Ollie, in our kids' ministry who had been in state care most of his life. His mother committed suicide and his dad was in and out of jail. I decided my weekly goal was to connect with Ollie. Every Sunday I would make sure I spoke words of encouragement to him and every Monday would send him a letter in the mail. One Sunday I noticed him sitting on the floor at the back separate from the other children. He had a pile of papers that he had spread out in front of him.

I watched as he picked the papers up one at a time, pretended to read them, and then placed them back in line on the floor. He refused to participate in the program. All he wanted to do was look at his papers.

Concerned, I sat down on the floor next to him trying to assess the situation. As I went over to say hello, I noticed my handwriting on some of the papers.

"Hi Ollie," I said. "What have you got there?" And then it hit me. They were all the letters I had sent him throughout the term. My eyes filled with tears as he looked at me, holding a letter smeared by the rain and said, "These are my very special letters."

Billy went on to explain that years later, Ollie was admitted to a children's psychiatric hospital, and though visitors weren't ordinarily permitted, she was given special permission to visit with Ollie because she had connected with him. Billy summed up the experience:

What a privilege to be able to connect with a child whose world is in chaos and remind him how special he is to God and how loved he is.[9]

Never underestimate the power of connection and the impact you can make simply by working to create an experience that others enjoy.

CONNECTING WITH PEOPLE AT ALL LEVELS

CONNECTING PRACTICE: Connectors create an experience everyone enjoys.

KEY CONCEPT: Work to create the right experience for your communication setting.

CONNECTING ONE-ON-ONE

When people enjoy a one-on-one communication experience, it is usually because a sense of intimacy has been created. That doesn't necessarily mean a romantic intimacy; it just means a connection created by honest communication that benefits both parties. Work to create that by doing one of the suggestions in the chapter, such as asking questions, using humor, or telling stories.

CONNECTING IN A GROUP

The experience that people usually enjoy most in a group setting is teamwork. As a communicator, if you can help people to have a sense of shared accomplishment, the participants will feel connected to you and to one another. The next time you're responsible for leading a group, ask them to accomplish some enjoyable task together. Make sure everyone gets involved. Then observe how it impacts the energy level and rapport of the group.

CONNECTING WITH AN AUDIENCE

When people are part of an audience listening to a communicator, they want to be entertained. Try using some of the many techniques I shared in the chapter the next time you communicate in front of an audience. In particular, use stories as part of communication. Even a dry report or highly factual presentation can be enlivened with a good story. (Perhaps those kinds of communication have the greatest need for a good story.)

If you haven't used stories in the past, try using them from now on when you connect with others. If you already use stories, think about ways you can improve your storytelling. Here are some tips from Martin Thielen, who attended the National Storytelling Festival in Jonesborough, Tennessee. He observed that the best presenters exhibited the following:

- ENTHUSIASM. The storytellers obviously enjoyed what they were doing, expressing themselves with joy and vitality.

- ANIMATION. The presentations were marked by lively facial expressions and gestures.

- AUDIENCE PARTICIPATION. Almost every storyteller involved the audience in some way, asking listeners to sing, clap, repeat phases, or do sign language.

- SPONTANEITY. Although the stories were memorized, storytellers responded freely to listeners.

- No Notes. This was truly an oral event. Storytellers didn't read their stories; they told them, which allowed for eye contact.

- Humor. Humor was interjected even in serious or sad stories.

Which of these can you use to enliven your communication?

9

CONNECTORS INSPIRE PEOPLE

Bill Hybels, the founder of Willow Creek Community Church in Chicago, hosts a Leadership Summit every year that seventy thousand people attend either in person or via satellite link. It is always a powerful and impacting event for church leaders, and I have had the privilege of speaking at it from time to time. In 2008, when Bill spoke during the closing session, his talk was on the importance of leaders inspiring others. He started his session by asking the following:

How much does it really matter if someone is highly motivated in their work, and in their life? Some of my research on how much motivation really matters was astounding to me. . . . Lots of studies that I read tossed around numbers like 40 percent or even higher when they compared the performance of motivated employees versus unmotivated employees. A 40 percent performance differential; staggering to me. I read one study that said motivated employees are 87 percent less likely to leave an organization compared to an unmotivated employee . . . Lots of studies that I read said that people who are motivated at work call in with dramatically fewer sick days, dramatically fewer insurance claims, less employee theft, fewer wasted hours, the list went on and on . . . There's a huge difference in the outcome, the deliverables, the achievements of motivated people versus unmotivated people. But you all kind of know this from personal experience; you know how much more you will give if someone inspires you.

There's no doubt about it: everyone benefits from motivation. Everyone wants to be inspired.

> *"Motivated employees are 87 percent less likely to leave an organization compared to an unmotivated employee."*
>
> —BILL HYBELS

As I look back on my life, I can see that my energy for my work has often been dependent upon the inspirational qualities of the person who led it. It goes all the way back to grammar school. I worked harder on my schoolwork in the fifth grade under Mr. Horton than I did in the sixth grade under Mrs. Webb. It was true in junior high and high school. I played basketball with greater intensity under Coach Neff than I did under Coach Shaw. And as a working adult, the same was true. I committed more time to the vision of Tom Phillippe than I did for other leaders in the same department. And I have given more money to the nonprofit organization led by Tom

Mullins than to other organizations that possess a similar mission. In every case, what made the difference was inspiration. Some people inspire us more than others do.

It All Adds up to Inspiration

For years I have studied leaders and speakers who inspire and connect with people. When someone begins to communicate with others, the first thing people do is start asking questions at a subconscious level. They want to know what's in it for them. They want to know if the speaker is credible. But they also care about *how* the person communicates with them.

As I have watched effective communicators inspire people, I have come to the conclusion that there is a kind of formula, which I call the Inspiration Equation, that comes into play. It works like this:

What They Know + What They See + What They Feel = Inspiration

When these three factors come into play and a communicator is able to bring them into alignment, it creates a synergy that inspires people. And from that place of inspiration, you can often lead people to take action. Let's take a look at each of these three pieces of the Inspiration Equation.

What People Need to Know

When non-connecting speakers think about what their listeners need to know, they focus on information. That's not what I'm talking about here. In the context of connecting, people need to know you're on their side. Greek philosopher Aristotle understood this and commented on it in *The Rhetoric.* In the context of persuasion, he identified the most important element as *pathos,* the communicators' ability to connect with the feelings, desires, wishes, fears, and passions of their listeners. It's a way of giving people reassurance, of letting them know they can trust you, of telling them that they should listen to you. How do you communicate that? I believe it boils down to two things:

PEOPLE NEED TO KNOW THAT YOU UNDERSTAND THEM AND ARE FOCUSED ON THEM

How inspired are you by people who appear to be concerned only about themselves? Probably not at all. I can't think of a single connector who doesn't care about his listeners. Self-centered people don't usually connect.

If you're going to connect, people need to know that you understand them. They need to sense that you're there for them. Good communicators understand that people do things for their own reasons, not for the reasons of the person doing the talking. Accordingly, they focus on their listeners' needs, not their own.

People who connect understand the same thing that actress Lisa Kirk knew when she said, "A gossip is one who talks to you about others; a bore is one who talks to you about himself; and a brilliant conversationalist is one who talks to you about yourself."[1] That's what connectors do. They tell you about yourself. They speak your inspirational language.

Leaders and speakers who understand this can make quite an impact on people. For example, Henry J. Kaiser, a shipbuilder during World War II, used his understanding of people to inspire his workers to increase the company's production when the United States desperately needed more ships. What was their inspirational language at that time? Competition. So Kaiser told employees at his Richmond,

California, facility that he wanted to see if they could break shipbuilding records for the war effort. They were inspired, not only to work harder but also to give suggestions that improved production methods. As a result, they built Liberty ships in an astounding seventy-two days, while other shipyards took, on average, twice the time.

When people know you care about them and understand them, it makes a lasting impression. Lea Carey cherishes the first note she received from a former boss, whom she describes as the best leader she ever worked for. "When I look at his handwritten note after all of these years," she said, "my heart still jumps a beat or two—because he took the time."[2] And pastor Adam Henry will never forget the positive words spoken to his congregation by a former teacher: "Someday I'm going to be able to say, 'I taught this guy in my class.'" Adam and his wife were overwhelmed. "Here we were just a young ministry couple, and this highly regarded man we also deeply respected was saying that he would be proud to say he knew me. It still inspires me to think back to this. His words did something in my heart that is deeper than simply receiving a compliment."[3]

As you prepare to communicate to others, you must let them know that you understand them and want to help them. You must learn their inspirational language and speak it to them. How do you do that? By asking these questions:

What are they thinking? Before I communicate with people, I try to find out as much as I can about them. I want to learn about their organizational culture and values. I want to know about their responsibilities. I want to understand their dreams. Why? Because I want to know what they're thinking. It helps me to speak their inspirational language. Speakers too often have the attitude, *This is what I think; sit down, and listen.* Connectors have the attitude, *I will sit down and listen before I share what I think.*

> *"The most called-upon prerequisite of a friend is an accessible ear."*
>
> —MAYA ANGELOU

What are they saying? American poet and writer Maya Angelou noted, "The most called-upon prerequisite of a friend is an accessible ear." That is also a prerequisite of being an inspiring leader or communicator.

Good leaders are good listeners. To be most effective, they follow this pattern: listen, learn, and then lead. Good communicators act similarly. They listen to what people are saying. They listen to how they are saying it. They even listen for what's not being said. That's how they read people. It's how some are able to read a room before they get up to speak, and it impacts how they communicate. Even the right thing said in the wrong situation won't connect.

What are they doing? This final question can be answered by watching others. Whenever I walk into someplace where I am going to communicate, I watch to see what activities people are engaged in. I also look at people's body language and try to discern their attitudes and energy levels. Once again, this helps me to read the room before I speak.

Of course, watching people can also help you to connect with others one-on-one, not just at formal speaking engagements. Recently on a trip, I observed a flight attendant who displayed a desire to help passengers but who seemed really nervous. When he came to my seat, I asked him his name. He told me his name was Tim, and he confided that he was a new flight attendant.

As he went on to assist other passengers, I decided to write him a note of encouragement. After I gave it to him, I watched as he went to his station and read it. I then saw him give it to another flight attendant, and she read it. A few minutes later she came to my seat and said, "Mr. Maxwell, it took you five minutes to give him something he will keep for a lifetime." Often it doesn't take a big thing to encourage or inspire others. All it takes is a little thing that lets someone know you understand and care about them.

PEOPLE NEED TO KNOW THAT YOU HAVE HIGH EXPECTATIONS OF THEM

President Abraham Lincoln, an incredible communicator, was known during the Civil War to attend a church not far from the White House on Wednesday nights. The preacher, Dr. Gurley, allowed the president to sit in the pastor's study with the door open to the chancel so he could listen to the sermon without having to interact with the crowd.

One Wednesday evening as Lincoln and a companion walked back to the White House after the sermon, the president's companion asked, "What did you think of tonight's sermon?"

"Well," Lincoln responded, "it was brilliantly conceived, biblical, relevant, and well presented."

"So it was a great sermon?"

"No," Lincoln replied. "It failed. It failed because Dr. Gurley did not ask us to do something great." Inspiring communicators always expect a lot from their listeners.

Every time I step in front of a group of people to communicate, I believe it will be a good experience for them and for me. Why is that? Because I believe the best in people, and I believe they can (and want to) change for the better. I'm convinced that all effective leaders and communicators possess this kind of positive quality. They believe they can help people do amazing things. It's as Steve Jobs, cofounder of Apple, said: "Management is about persuading people to do things they do not want to do, while leadership is about inspiring people to do things they never thought they could."

When I communicate with people, I do something that I call putting a 10 on their heads. By that I mean that I see everyone as having the potential to be a "10" on a scale of 1 to 10. One of the reasons I do this is that I'm naturally positive. I believe God created every person with value and incredible potential. But the other reason I do this is because I believe most of the time people respond to the expectations of others. If I see someone as a 5, I'll treat him or her as a 5 and speak to this person as a 5. And more than likely, after a while I'll convince this person to act as a 5. What's the value in that? However, if I see someone as a 10, he or she will sense that and is likely to respond in a positive way. If we treat people as who they can become, they will be inspired to rise to the level of our expectations.

> *"Management is about persuading people to do things they do not want to do, while leadership is about inspiring people to do things they never thought they could."*
>
> —STEVE JOBS

Of course, putting a high value on people can sometimes be taken to a comical extreme. Jacques Fortin explained that he shared with his wife the idea of putting a 10 on people's heads. A short time later, he returned from the grocery store and told her, "I had to give a woman a 20."

"Was she that good looking?" his wife asked.

"No, she was pregnant."[4]

Bart Looper wrote me to confirm the positive impact on others that our expectations can have. He explained, "I have a couple of employees who have been with me about three years. They are about

the same age and have a similar demeanor. I realize now that the reason that one of them is so far ahead of the other is due to me. Sometime in the last three years, I viewed one of them as a 10 and the other as a 5. I have treated them as such, and they have grown as such. Starting Monday morning, I am going to make sure that I treat, train, and share my vision equally with them because they both have the same potential. I just have to communicate it to them.[5]

It is always my intention to converse, write, and speak with high expectations for people. When I encourage people one-on-one, I believe the best about them. As I sit down to work on a book, I envision readers embracing what I say and becoming better people as a result. When I speak, I believe listeners will respond in a positive way. I am challenged to give my best to others so they will give the best of themselves. People respond positively to enthusiasm, not skepticism. They want our encouragement more than our expertise. Otherwise, we come across the way 1984 presidential candidate Walter Mondale did during his campaign. One journalist observed, "He is stirring up apathy all over the country."

Pastor and professor Calvin Miller expresses the way most audiences feel in his book *The Empowered Communicator*. When someone gets up to speak, what most listeners would like to say is this:

Promise me that I, who am riddled with inferiority, will at last believe in myself. I have always been afraid of heights. Challenge me with Everest. Promise me that after your words, I will be able to scale those icy walls and with God's help plant His mighty flag on the summit of all my doubts. Promise me that I at last will know who I am and what I was born to achieve. Promise all this and you shall have first my ear . . . and then my soul.

Everyone wants to be inspired. All people want someone to believe in them. They are waiting for someone to challenge, motivate, and encourage them to be all they can be. If you get an opportunity to communicate to others, why not be that someone who inspires them?

WHAT PEOPLE NEED TO SEE

Most people decide very quickly whether they will continue listening to you or simply "turn off" and stop paying attention. Often they make that decision based on what they see. Their perceptions begin at a surface level. Do you look pleasant? Do you smile? Are your posture and bearing positive? If there are no red flags for your listeners, then they are usually willing to give you enough time to prove yourself. Here's what they're looking for:

PEOPLE NEED TO SEE YOUR CONVICTION

Scottish philosopher and religious skeptic David Hume was once observed hurrying early one morning to hear evangelist George Whitefield preach. When someone asked where he was going and was told, "To hear George Whitefield," the questioner asked him if he believed what the evangelist preached.

"Certainly not!" Hume replied, "But Whitefield does, and I want to hear a man who does."[6]

Larry Phillips commented, "There is a noticeable difference between steel and tin—especially when hit. Genuine heartfelt convictions simply come across as 'words of steel.' There is a determined resolve in the tone. As communicators, we need to be reminded that we can't fake convictions! The audience will always discern the difference between words of steel and the sound of tin—no matter how hard the tin is hit!"[7]

Connectors who inspire others possess a conviction that far outweighs their words. What they communicate comes from deep within, from their inner core values. Their mission is to persuade, to change points of view. People can usually sense when speakers are simply conveying information versus when they are passionately communicating from the heart.

President Lyndon B. Johnson asserted, "What convinces is conviction. Believe in the argument you're advancing. If you don't, you're as good as dead. The other person will sense that something isn't there, and no chain of reasoning, no matter how logical or elegant or brilliant, will win your case for you." If the speaker doesn't have conviction about the subject of his or her message, why should the listeners?

PEOPLE NEED TO SEE YOUR CREDIBILITY

Many of my speaking engagements have been one-shot deals. I'm booked as a keynote speaker, and I get one forty-five-minute session to deliver the goods. However, because of my background as a minister, I've also had a lot of experience speaking to essentially the same people week after week for many years. But in both cases, listeners were looking for the same thing from me: credibility.

When people trust you, they will listen to you, and they will be open to being inspired by you. If you are a one-time speaker, people will often give you the benefit of the doubt, as long as your credentials are good. But if you're going to speak to the same people time and again, you have to work to maintain credibility.

PEOPLE NEED TO SEE EVIDENCE OF YOUR CHARACTER

In the end, people want to be able to trust the character of the person who is communicating to them. A trustworthy person's character does not stop when the words do. Rather, it continues in the conduct of his or her daily life. Perhaps that is why it's said that the mediocre teacher tells. The good teacher explains. The great teacher demonstrates. Ultimately, each of us should strive to *be* the message.

> *The mediocre teacher tells. The good teacher explains. The great teacher demonstrates.*

That was certainly true of Mohandas Gandhi in the independence movement in India. Gandhi inspired his people with his words. But he inspired them even more with his actions. His commitment to Indian independence and his example of non-violent protest rallied the nation to follow him in demanding their independence from Britain. That is the power of character. As author, speaker, and coach Brad Cork remarked, "Connecting has a lot to do with letting who you are influence everything you do."[8]

As I've already said, people often decide very quickly whether they want to listen to another person. They make that initial judgment based largely on superficial impressions. Their decision to *continue* listening is often based on a deeper perception related to the person's credibility. I'll address this in greater detail in the next chapter.

WHAT PEOPLE NEED TO FEEL

Making sure people know what they need to know is important for inspiring others. So is making sure they see what they need to see. But the most important factor in the Inspiration Equation is what they feel. If you leave that part out and you don't help people feel what they need to feel, they will never be inspired. Why? Because people will not always remember what you said or what you did, but they will always remember how you made them feel!

If you want to inspire people, there are three things you need in order to help them feel:

PEOPLE NEED TO FEEL YOUR PASSION FOR THE SUBJECT AND THEM

Vision without passion is a picture without possibilities. Vision alone does not inspire change. It must be strengthened by passion. History reveals many examples of this. Martin Luther King Jr. did not stand on the steps of the Lincoln Memorial and proclaim, "I have a plan." No logical strategy could have inspired people to stand up to oppression or to change the way they treated others. No, with the passion of someone who had suffered prejudice and dreamed of equality, King said, "I have a dream!"

In *A Sense of Urgency*, author, professor, and leadership expert John Kotter describes King's communication thus:

> *People will not always remember what you said or what you did, but they will always remember how you made them feel!*

A mind-driven case for change could easily be made, and was made by many people at the time: treatment of blacks was inconsistent with some of the country's most long-cherished values, and inconsistencies have pernicious effects; wasting black talent undermined the country's interest; angry conflict among blacks and whites wasted resources and hurt people;

un-Christian behavior toward blacks undermined Christianity itself and its foundation that served society. King's speech addressed all these points briefly, but mostly it pounded away at people's gut-level feelings with poetic rhetoric and passionate words about justice and morality. He hit hearts in a way that converted anger and anxiety into a commitment to move, do the right thing, and now. He hit hearts in a way that converted complacency into real urgency. Tens of millions of people not at the rally that day saw the speech on TV or heard it on the radio. Urgency went up, essential action followed, and legislation that would probably have failed the year before was passed into law.

Passion is powerful. It supersedes mere spoken words. Joyce McMurran remarked, "I am convinced that your passion and purpose will always show through and make an impact no matter what you are doing."[9] Isn't that true? The message may be spoken or written, but to be inspiring, it must be birthed in the passion of the person communicating. This is why Horst Schultze, founding president and former chief operating officer of the Ritz-Carlton Hotel Company, stated, "You are nothing unless it comes from your heart. Passion, caring, really looking to create excellence. If you perform functions only and go to work only to do processes, then you are effectively retired. And it scares me—most people I see, by age twenty-eight are retired."

> *Vision without passion is a picture without possibilities.*

Years ago when I lived in San Diego, a friend named Geri Stevens was the head of the jury selection process in the judicial department of the city. Each Monday as a new pool of potential jurors arrived at court, she addressed them to talk about their responsibilities.

If you have ever sat in a room of potential jurors, you know that it's not a cheerful place. The room is usually filled with unhappy people who are not inspired to be there. One Monday morning after months of Geri prodding me, she finally convinced me to attend one of these sessions. And I was surprised by what happened.

Geri stood before her unreceptive audience with an air of excitement and said, "This will be one of the most wonderful weeks of your lives." That got everybody's attention. She proceeded to talk passionately for the next forty-five minutes about the greatness of America and the right of each citizen to have a fair trial. She explained to the jurors how their decisions would make a difference and that they were examples of why America is a nation coveted and admired by others. At the close of her inspiring talk, the potential jurors gave her a standing ovation! Her passion had transferred to them. They were inspired, and they were actually looking forward to being selected to serve on a jury.

When you speak, do you have passion? Real passion is more than just an emotion that you whip up to get listeners excited. It comes from a much deeper place than that. If you're not sure, the next time before you speak to people, ask yourself these four questions:

1. Do I believe what I say?

2. Has it changed me?

3. Do I believe it will help others?

4. Have I seen it change others?

If you can answer yes to those questions, you'll do more than just light a fire under people. You will build a fire within them! If you have that fire, it will ignite in others.

PEOPLE NEED TO FEEL YOUR CONFIDENCE IN YOURSELF AND THEM

As I've said, passion has great value because it motivates people. Why? Because it helps them to say yes to the question, "Will it be worth it?" But passion alone isn't enough. People must also feel your confidence because confidence is what inspires them to say yes to the question, "Can I do it?" Inspiration comes to people when they can readily answer yes to both of these questions. That's when they become willing to make changes that positively impact their lives.

Have you ever listened to a speaker who lacked confidence and announced that he or she was nervous? How did that make you feel? Confident? Probably not. More than likely, you began to worry about how the session was going to go. Presenters who create worry in their listeners don't inspire great confidence. In fact, they don't inspire anything.

As a communicator, you have to feel good about yourself in order to help others feel good about themselves. If I'm confident about myself and tell you that I'm confident in you and your ability to do something, you are more likely to find what I say credible.

Some leaders and speakers naturally exude confidence and make others feel confident about themselves. President Franklin Roosevelt was said to be one such person. In her biography of Franklin and Eleanor Roosevelt, *No Ordinary Time*, Doris Kearns Goodwin notes that Roosevelt wasn't our most intelligent president. He surrounded himself with people who were more educated, gifted, and knowledgeable. However, what he had was an incredible confidence in himself and in the American people.

Roosevelt's White House Counsel, Sam Rosenman, observed that the president had the ability to make others believe in themselves. He said that people exposed to Roosevelt's confidence "begin to feel it and take part in it, to rejoice in it—and to return it tenfold by their own confidence." And Labor Secretary Francis Perkins said that she often "came away from an interview with the President feeling better, not because he had solved any problems . . . but because he had made me feel more cheerful, stronger, more determined."

If you're not overflowing with natural confidence, then don't lose heart. You can still learn to help your listeners feel more confident about themselves if you approach communication the right way. In their book *Influencer*, Patterson, Grenny, Maxfield, McMillan, and Switzler tell the story of a group of American auto workers who visited a Japanese auto plant and, upon returning home, wanted to tell their coworkers that they all needed to work harder and faster. The story shows that nearly anyone can learn to connect better with people. Here is an excerpt, explaining the workers' multiple attempts at communication, and how they finally figured out how to connect with their audience and help them feel confidence in not only the speaker but also themselves:

> They gathered a group of their peers together and announced their finding—their competitors actually did produce 40 percent more per employee by working faster and more consistently. At the end of this rather terse and unpopular announcement, the members of the task force were booed off the stage by their own union brothers and sisters.

Undaunted, the world travelers brought another group together and told them the shortened version of what had happened. More boos. Finally, the team leader selected the best storyteller and set him loose on the next assembly of employees. He didn't ruin the message by quickly cutting to the chase—"Workers unite or we're dead!" Instead, this gifted storyteller took a full ten minutes to narrate in vivid detail what had taken place.

The members of the task force had arrived in Japan, and to a person they were absolutely certain the foreigners they would soon observe would put on a show. Sure enough, they did (jeers). But the task force wasn't fooled (cheers). Next, the storyteller related how they had sneaked into the plant after hours and spied on the enemy (more cheers). But wait a second; the employees were working even faster (silence). This was depressing. If the Japanese workers continued to outperform the American workers, the Japanese companies could keep their costs down and dominate the market. American companies would downsize, and American workers would lose their jobs.

After they spied on the Japanese workers, the members of the task force returned to their hotel and tried to figure out how to beat their competitors at their own game. Then it hit them. Why not work on the Japanese line and see if they could handle the jobs? For the next couple of days they stepped into a variety of the jobs on the Japanese production line and performed them quite readily. It was work, but nothing they couldn't handle (more cheers). And finally the punch line: "If we take the right steps, we can take our fate back into our own hands and save our jobs" (raucous applause).

The storytelling auto worker approached communication with confidence, and he helped his fellow workers feel confidence in themselves. That is always a necessary component for communication that inspires.

PEOPLE NEED TO FEEL YOUR GRATITUDE FOR THEM

The final component needed to inspire people is gratitude—yours for your listeners. And that is as it should be. As a communicator, you should be grateful that people are willing to give you their ear. You should be grateful if they stay and continue listening to you. And you should be even more grateful if they are so inspired that they take to heart what you have to say.

> *Of all the virtues, gratitude is probably the most neglected and least expressed.*

I believe that of all the virtues, gratitude is probably the most neglected and least expressed. Too many people are like the son of the immigrant shopkeeper who came to his father, complaining, "Dad, I don't understand how you run this store. You keep your accounts payable in a cigar box. Your accounts receivable are on a spindle. All your cash is in the register. You never know what your profits are."

"Son," answered the shopkeeper, "let me tell you something. When I arrived in this land, all I owned was the pants I was wearing. Now your sister is an art teacher. Your brother is a doctor. You are a CPA. Your mother and I own a house and a car and this little store. Add that all up and subtract the pants and there is your profit."

Gladys Stern observed, "Silent gratitude isn't much good to anyone." That is so true. That's why I work at cultivating a heart of gratitude, and I make an effort to express gratitude continually. I try to be grateful for the small things. And for the big ones, sometimes I have to do something highly intentional to express my gratitude.

> *"Silent gratitude isn't much good to anyone."*
>
> —GLADYS STERN

That was the case in the summer of 2008. As the ten-year anniversary of my heart attack approached, I was feeling especially grateful for my life and for the doctors whose work saved me. To say thank you, Margaret and I decided to have a gratitude dinner with them and their spouses to celebrate the additional ten years of life I had enjoyed (so far). We made arrangements to host the dinner with some friends at their home, arranged to have a chef prepare a five-course meal, and I wrote something special for the occasion.

The evening turned out to be an unforgettable experience. After a couple of hours of great food and conversation, I read them the following letter:

Doctors John Bright Cage and Jeff Marshall,

Ten years ago I had a heart attack. God used both of you to spare my life. This is a letter of gratitude. The words in this letter are from my heart. They must be written as a tangible way of giving thanks to you. I believe that silent gratitude isn't much good to anyone.

Your lives have been dedicated to helping people. No doubt over the years many people have been given a second chance to live. For ten years I have been living my "second-chance" life. Because of God's goodness and your giftedness, allow me to briefly share what has happened during this time:

- I have enjoyed my extra ten years with Margaret and my family.

- Five grandchildren have been born and stolen my heart.

- Thirty-eight books have been written that have sold over fifteen million copies.

- Amazon.com inducted me into their Hall of Fame.

- I have been named the "World's #1 Leadership Guru."

- Three Leadership events have been founded by me:

  > Catalyst—A young leaders' conference averaging 12,000 per event
  > Maximum Impact Simulcast—which reaches 100,000 people each year
  > Exchange—a high-level executive experience

- Two of my companies have experienced wonderful growth:

  > INJOY Stewardship Services has partnered with 4,000 churches and raised over $4 billion.
  > EQUIP has trained 3 million leaders in 113 countries.

- It has been my privilege to speak for the United Nations, West Point, NASA, the CIA, and many Fortune 500 companies.

- Most important, over 7,500 people have received Christ through my teaching!

First Samuel 2:9 says, "God protectively cares for his faithful friends, step by step." Dr. Cage, it was no "accident" when you handed me your business card and said, "John, God has asked me to take care of you. Call me at anytime if you need help." Dr. Marshall, it was no "accident" that you met me at the hospital with your team and said, "We are here to take care of you; everything's going to be fine."

For the last ten years I have continually expressed to God my gratefulness for both of you. Tonight I give you this letter and say with great love and appreciation, "Thank you!"

Your friend,

John

Margaret then gave each of them the letter I had just read. I was in tears, and so were they. For the next thirty minutes, we exchanged expressions of love and hugs. The experience was indescribable. And as much as I tried, I still couldn't adequately express the gratitude I felt.

To help listeners feel passionate, confident, and inspired, you must express gratitude. And to do that, you must first be a grateful person. You cannot give what you do not have. The good news is that gratitude is a quality that can be cultivated—no matter your circumstances. Each of us should strive to be more like Matthew Henry, who lived in the eighteenth century. When he was robbed, he wrote the following in his diary: "Let me be thankful first because I was never robbed before; second, although they took my purse, they did not take my life; third, because although they took my all, it was not much; and fourth, because it was I who was robbed, not I who robbed."

ACTION—INSPIRATION AT THE HIGHEST LEVEL

When a communicator puts these three things together:

What They Know + What They See + What They Feel

then the result is inspiration. It's what Jerry Weissman, author of *Presenting to Win,* calls the "aha moment." Weissman wrote:

> Aha! would be represented by the image of a light bulb clicking on above your audience's heads. It's that satisfying moment of understanding and agreement that occurs when an idea from one person's mind has been successfully communicated into another's. This process is a mystery as old as language itself and almost as profound as love; the ability of humans, using only words and symbols, to understand one another and find common ground in an idea, a plan, a dream.
>
> Maybe you've enjoyed moments like this in your past experiences as a presenter, speaker, salesperson, or communicator, moments when you saw the light bulb go on, as eyes made contact, smiles spread, and heads nodded. Aha! is the moment when you know your audience is ready to march to your beat.[10]

Some communicators stop there. They encourage people, make them feel good, help them to feel confident, but then they never lead them to action. What a tragedy! It's not enough to help someone feel good. Understanding changes *minds.* Action changes *lives.* If you really want to help others, you need to take your communication to the next level—which is to call people to action. As Maribeth Hickman commented, "Connection provides the bridge between 'this is how' and 'begin now.'"[11] When do inspired people take action? When you do two things:

SAY THE RIGHT WORDS AT THE RIGHT TIME

To take people from inspiration to action, you must put together the right words and deliver them at the right moment. Good leaders understand the importance of timing. In my book *The 21 Irrefutable Laws of Leadership*, I've written about the Law of Timing, which says, "When to lead is as important as what to do and where to go." Timing is often the difference between success and failure in any endeavor. Good communicators understand the importance of the right words. Novelist Joseph Conrad observed, "Words have set whole nations in motion and upheaved the dry, hard ground on which rests our social fabric. Give me the right word and the right accent, and I will move the world." When you put both together, it is powerful!

In his book *Am I Making Myself Clear?* Terry Felber writes about how Franklin Roosevelt prepared his speech to Congress following the bombing of Pearl Harbor. He explains that in Roosevelt's first draft, Roosevelt dictated, "Yesterday, December 7, 1941, a day that will live in world history, the United States was suddenly and deliberately attacked. . . ." After a secretary typed out the five-hundred-word message, he looked it over and made only one change. He crossed out the words "world history" and replaced them with a single, well chosen word: "infamy." Felber wrote, "As we all know, 'a day that will live in infamy' are some of the most famous words ever spoken by a United States president. The right choice of words created a message that will live forever in history."

That phrase, delivered as it was the day after the attack on Pearl Harbor, set the nation into motion. Thousands of young men enlisted in the military after hearing them. And the American people girded themselves for war.

GIVE PEOPLE AN ACTION PLAN

There is an old story about a farmer who asked his neighbor, "Are you going to attend the new county agent's classes next week?" His neighbor replied, "Shucks. I already know a whole lot more about farming than I'm doing." That's the way most people are: their knowledge far outweighs their follow-through. Good communicators help people to overcome that tendency.

I think of myself as a motivational teacher, not a motivational speaker. What's the difference between the two? A motivational speaker makes you feel good, but the next day you're not sure why. A motivational teacher makes you feel good, and the next day you know why and take action. In other words, the first kind of communicator wants you to *feel* good, and the second wants you to *do* good.

I once read the statistic that 95 percent of the people in an audience understand what's being communicated and agree with the speaker's point of view. However, they do not know how to apply what's being said to their lives. Isn't that amazing? That's why I usually give people an action plan. It's also one of the reasons I began writing books and offering audio lessons. I wanted people to have something they could take away with them that will help them on an ongoing basis. My desire is to help people move from "know how" to "do now."

Connectors inspire people to move from "know how" to "do now."

Many times I offer very specific steps that my listeners can take. But even for a message that is very broad or that doesn't lend itself

223

to concrete steps, I still recommend an action plan to people based on the word ACT. I tell them,

- Put a letter "A" beside those things you learned that you need to Apply.

- Put a letter "C" beside those things you learned that you need to Change.

- Put a letter "T" beside those things you learned that you need to Teach.

Then I encourage them to pick one item to take action on within the next twenty-four hours, and to share the most important thing they learned with another person. This may seem simple, but if applied, it can be life changing.

Make a Commitment to Continually Inspire Others

Norm Lawson tells the story of a rabbi and a soap maker who went for a walk together. The soap maker said, "What good is religion? Look at all the trouble and misery of the world! Still there, even after years—thousands of years—of teaching about goodness and truth and peace. Still there, after all the prayers and sermons and teachings. If religion is good and true, why should this be?"

The rabbi said nothing. They continued walking until they noticed a child playing in the gutter.

Then the rabbi said, "Look at that child. You say that soap makes people clean, but see the dirt on that youngster. Of what good is soap? With all the soap in the world, over all these years, the child is still filthy. I wonder how effective soap is, after all!"

The soap maker protested, "But, Rabbi, soap cannot do any good unless it is used!"

"Exactly," replied the rabbi.

Raymond Master commented, "Our society seems to go from inspiration to inspiration, looking for the next thing that makes them feel good, but doing very little about it."[12] How sad. According to some scholars, there hasn't always been such a divide between understanding and action. One linguist says that in up to twenty primitive languages, the words for "hearing" and "doing" are the same word. Only in our modern context have we divided them. As communicators, we need to bring those two ideas back together for our listeners. And that requires a commitment to continually connecting with others, inspiring them, and encouraging them to take action.

> *"The way I like to measure greatness is . . . How many people can you make want to be better?"*
>
> —WILL SMITH

Actor Will Smith once said, "The way I like to measure greatness is: How many people do you affect? In your time on earth, how many people can you affect? How many people can you make want to be better? Or how many people can you inspire?" In the end, what good is our communication if its impact ends the moment we stop speaking?

The true purpose of inspiration isn't applause. Its value isn't in the wonder it may create or the positive feelings it can evoke in others. The true test of inspiration is action. That is what makes a difference.

If you desire to connect with others, you must strive to inspire people. But don't do that to make yourself or others feel better. Do it to make the world better. If you can inspire others, making the world better is within your reach.

CONNECTING WITH PEOPLE AT ALL LEVELS

CONNECTING PRACTICE: Connectors inspire people.

KEY CONCEPT: What people remember most is how you make them feel.

CONNECTING ONE-ON-ONE

All three factors in the Inspiration Equation come into play when inspiring people, but they have different values in different communication settings. One-on-one, what has the greatest weight is what people see. Who you really are inspires (or discourages) the people closest to you. You can't hide that. Character, above everything else, is what will make the biggest impression on people at this level.

What qualities help people to connect with you? Here is what they want to see:

- A heart to serve—people need to know that you want to serve them.

- A person of good values—show your values by words and action.

- A helping hand—add value to others and always try to lift them up.

- A caring spirit—people don't care how much you know until they know how much you care.

- A believing attitude—people migrate to those who believe in them.

CONNECTING IN A GROUP

What people know about you counts the most when inspiring people in a group. They want to know what you've done. That is what gives you the most credibility. If people know and respect your accomplishments, and you believe in them, then they will believe in themselves and be inspired to perform.

People in a group want to know . . .

- that you will go first and lead by example,

- that you will only ask them to do what you have done or are willing to do,

- that you will teach them to do what you have already done,

- that their success is more important to you than your success,

- that they will get credit for their accomplishments, and

- that you will celebrate their success.

CONNECTING WITH AN AUDIENCE

The most important aspect of communication when trying to connect with an audience is how you make them feel. Most times, they can't really know the speaker and anything about his or her character from a distance. They may have been told information about the speaker's achievements, but they can't be sure about them. What they have is their reaction to the few minutes the speaker communicates onstage. If they feel good, they feel connected. If they don't, they don't. So if you're preparing to speak to an audience, be sure you try to connect with them on an emotional level. The following will help you do that:

- They should see that you enjoy being with them and want to help them.

- They should feel that you are their friend.

- They should feel that you are authentic and vulnerable—not perfect, but growing.

- They should feel you are conversing with them, not talking down to them.

- They should feel that you believe in them and they can believe in themselves.

10

CONNECTORS LIVE WHAT
THEY COMMUNICATE

Usually when someone new steps into a leadership position, the people impacted have hope. They want their leader to do well. And if the leader has good communication skills and is able to connect, then people listen, believe, and follow. But this honeymoon doesn't last long.

In the first six months of a relationship—whether it's personal or professional, one-to-one or leader-to-follower—we focus on a person's communication ability in order to make judgments about him. Haven't you found that to be true? If people don't communicate well, we have doubt. But if they're good at connecting, we have hope. For example, when we have a new boss who speaks well and casts a compelling vision, we buy in. When we connect well with a new neighbor or coworker, we feel that we have a new friend. When we meet the person we end up marrying, we think everything will always be wonderful.

> *Credibility is currency for leaders and communicators. With it, they are solvent; without it, they are bankrupt.*

And for most people, the honeymoon is wonderful. But after the honeymoon comes the marriage. Sometimes that, too, is wonderful, but sometimes it's not.

What makes the difference? Credibility! Here's how this works in any kind of relationship:

The first six months—communication overrides credibility.

After six months—credibility overrides communication.

When a person is credible, the longer the time, the better it gets. For someone who lacks credibility, the longer the time, the worse it gets. Credibility is currency for leaders and communicators. With it, they are solvent; without it, they are bankrupt. With credibility, leaders continue to connect with people. Without it, they disconnect.

THE TRUST TEST

In January 2009, Barack Obama took office as the forty-fourth president of the United States. As I write this, he has been in office for less than six months. Everyone still has hope. The president is a good communicator. He knows how to connect with people. He did very well on the campaign trail. Carl M. Cannon, author of "Ten Reasons Why Obama Won," wrote of Obama, "He combined, in some odd alchemy, Kennedy's discipline as a campaigner, Bill Clinton's gift of gab, and Ronald Reagan's optimism and Teflon quality."[1] He really was quite exceptional in his campaign for the presidency.

By the time you are reading this, enough time will have passed, and the jury will be in. You will either acknowledge that President Obama has developed credibility, proven himself, and led well—or you will say that his communication outweighed his credibility and he didn't deliver on what he said he would do. That's the way credibility works, not just for him but for every politician, every leader, every parent. As time goes by, the way people live outweighs the words they use. If they live well, time is their friend.

Credibility is all about trust. Stephen M. R. Covey wrote in *The Speed of Trust* about the impact of credibility in business. He asserts, "Trust means confidence," because trust erases worry and frees you to get on with other matters. "Low trust," he writes, "is an unseen cost in life and business, because it creates hidden agendas and guarded communication, thereby slowing decision-making. A lack of trust stymies innovation and productivity. Trust, on the other hand, produces speed because it feeds collaboration, loyalty and ultimately, results."

> *As time goes by, the way people live outweighs the words they use.*

Trust plays the same role in all relationships, and it always impacts communication. To be an effective connector over the long haul, you have to establish credibility by living what you communicate. If you don't, you undermine trust, people disconnect from you, and they stop listening. The bottom line is that the effectiveness of the communication relies more on the character of the messenger than on the content of the message.

YOU ARE YOUR MESSAGE

One of the things that I've found very frustrating is the actions of many players in Major League Baseball. I grew up loving baseball and was a big fan of the Cincinnati Reds. In recent years, players have been breaking time-honored records, but they've been doing it by using steroids. One seemingly great player after another has been charged with using steroids. Some have admitted the double life they've been living. Others have denied it or taken the fifth. Baseball is a game of statistics. If the statistics aren't credible because of players' use of performance-enhancing substances, the game has been irreparably damaged.

Whether or not you intend to be, you are the message you communicate to others. That determines whether other people want to connect with you. Even the most skilled performer can't keep up a facade forever. Eventually who you really are will show through—onstage, at work, or at home. So if you want to connect well with people, you must become the kind of person you would like to connect with. How you portray yourself, what you communicate, and how you live need to be consistent. Here are my suggestions for making that happen.

CONNECT WITH YOURSELF

The relationships we have with others are largely determined by the relationships we have with ourselves. If we are not accepting of who we are, if we are uncomfortable with ourselves as people, if we don't know our own strengths and weaknesses, then the attempts we make to connect with others will usually misfire. How can you connect with others on common ground if you don't know and like yourself? How can you see others clearly if you have an unclear view of yourself? Once we know ourselves and like ourselves and feel comfortable with ourselves, then we are open to knowing others, liking them, and feeling comfortable with them. And then we have the potential to connect with them.

The first step toward connecting with ourselves is knowing ourselves, and that comes from self-assessment. We need to become self-aware. Take tests to learn your strengths. Set aside time to reflect, journal, and pray. Talk to others about your weaknesses. You have to be intentional. The irony is that we need to spend some time focusing on ourselves so we can become free to take the focus off of ourselves and put it on others.

The second step comes from liking ourselves, and that comes from self-talk. Master motivator Zig Ziglar says, "The most influential person who will talk to you all day, is you. So, you should be very careful what you say to you." If you are constantly saying critical and negative things about yourself internally, you won't be confident with yourself or with others. You have to be positive. That doesn't mean denying wrongdoing or glossing over problems or mistakes. It means maintaining a realistic but positive outlook on life.

Recently I was having dinner with a friend who leads a successful organization in Arkansas, and one of the things he said as we talked was, "John, of all the people I know, you are the most comfortable in your own skin." I took it as a high compliment. I am comfortable with myself. I know who I am. I'm not a well-rounded person. My strengths are few—I believe I have only four (leadership, communication, creating, and networking). My weaknesses are many. I try to be honest about my weaknesses, focus on using my strengths, and have integrity in every area of my life. What else can I do?

If you've never taken the time to connect with yourself, I hope you will do so beginning today. It's not a selfish act. I believe you will be able to do what you were created for only if you know and connect with yourself. And you will also be able to better connect with others and add value to them if you know what you do and don't have to offer.

RIGHT YOUR WRONGS

As I mentioned, to connect with people you must have credibility. But how much credibility can you maintain when you make mistakes? That depends on how you respond.

Failure to admit mistakes

causes

the message to be questioned

which causes

the integrity of the leader to be questioned!

Everybody makes mistakes. I've made mistakes as a leader, communicator, husband, and parent. To be human is to mess up; to connect, you must fess up.[2] That's how you maintain your integrity and regain your credibility. You must be willing to:

Acknowledge Your Mistakes. When decisions don't turn out the way they were intended to, you owe people an explanation. One of the things I've admired in the first few months of Obama's presidency is his willingness to admit mistakes. When the cabinet nomination of Tom Daschle blew up, President Obama said simply, "I screwed up." I admire that in a leader.

> *To be human is to mess up; to connect, you must fess up.*

Apologize. When your actions hurt others, you need to admit that what you did was wrong and say you are sorry. That's usually very painful in the moment, but not only is it the right thing to do, it can actually shorten the agony you feel and help you put the incident behind you. That's why we should take the advice of Thomas Jefferson on this subject. He remarked, "If you have to eat crow, eat it while it's young and tender."[3]

Make Amends. And of course, if it is within your power, you need to find ways to make it up to the people you have wronged. Not long ago I had to do this after making a terrible mistake during a return speaking engagement for an organization. While I was speaking, I could tell from the audience's response that something wasn't right, but I couldn't figure out what it was. Not until after I left the stage did it occur to me that I might have given essentially the same talk that I had done previously. I called my assistant, and she confirmed that my suspicion was correct. I immediately went to my host, apologized to him, and asked if I could apologize to the audience the next day. He was very gracious about it. I then offered to return the next year, pay all my own expenses, and speak for him again at no cost. I thought that was the right thing to do under the circumstances. I couldn't turn back the clock, but I could do everything in my power to make amends.

BE ACCOUNTABLE

As you've probably already gathered, I enjoy studying leaders, and U.S. presidents are of particular interest to me. Out of that interest, I have a question for you. What do Theodore Roosevelt, Franklin Delano Roosevelt, Harry Truman, and Ronald Reagan all have in common? If you've read about them, you know they were all very different. They were from different political parties. They had different philosophies and leadership styles. But what did they have in common? They were seen to have delivered on their promises.

What is one of the best compliments you can give to another person? I believe it's this: "I can count on you." That's why I included the Law of Countability in *The 17 Indisputable Laws of Teamwork*. It says teammates must be able to count on each other when it counts. But that need for us to be "countable" and accountable to one another is

> *When you make a commitment, you create hope. When you keep a commitment, you create trust.*

true for any relationship—not just those on a team. This is why: When you make a commitment, you create hope. When you keep a commitment, you create trust.

In general, we most often need accountability in our areas of weakness. We're fine when it comes to our strengths. We like working in our strengths. We are most likely to follow through in our areas of strength. People expect that of us. However, when it comes to our weaknesses, we need to allow others to ask us questions, to challenge us. If we don't, we are prone to get off track.

LEAD THE WAY YOU LIVE

Author and speaker Jim Rohn observed, "You cannot speak that which you do not know. You cannot share that which you do not feel. You cannot translate that which you do not have. And you cannot give that which you do not possess. To give it and to share it, and for it to be effective, you first need to have it." That means you first need to live it!

In leadership, the importance of modeling what you communicate is clear. History is filled with examples of leaders who made an impact by being in front and saying, in essence, "Follow me." Fred A. Manske Jr. points out in *Secrets of Effective Leadership*:

- General Robert E. Lee made it a practice to visit his troops the night before a major battle, doing so at the expense of getting sleep himself.

- General George S. Patton was often seen riding in the lead tank of his armor units, inspiring his men to fight.

- The Duke of Wellington, who defeated Napoleon at Waterloo, believed that Napoleon's presence on the battlefield was worth 40,000 soldiers.

People who live their message, who lead the way they live, who have integrity between words and action, are different from others who don't. They are connectors, in part, because of how they live. Where some people see a message as *a lesson to be given*, connectors look at a message as *a life to be lived*. Where some offer a message that is an *exception* to how they live, connectors communicate messages that are *extensions* of how they live. For some communicators, *content* is the most important issue. For connectors, credibility is the most important issue.

Teacher Lindsay Fawcett commented, "I've heard that the first job you take as a teacher influences the rest of your career. Sometimes it is overwhelming, and no one is willing to help you get on your feet (as with my friend who no longer teaches), and sometimes the administration lifts you up and encourages you to reach your potential. I experienced the latter," said Lindsay about her first job out of college in Minneapolis. "My principal and ESL coordinator encouraged me to lead and try new things and they trusted my judgment. I felt so loved and appreciated that all I wanted to do was to prove them right. They know how to connect with their staff, and this made working for them feel like I was with family."[4] Credible leadership makes a huge impact on people in an organization.

If you aren't willing to try to live something, you probably shouldn't try to communicate it. That doesn't mean you have to try to be perfect because, of course, you can't be. It just means you have to strive to *be* what you call others to be. Otherwise, you have no credibility, and your leadership is in trouble. As blogger and student minister

Adam Jones put it, "Leading with a lack of integrity is choosing to fail before taking your first step."[5]

TELL THE TRUTH

A woman accompanied her very sick husband to the doctor's office. After the examination, the doctor asked the man to go out to the waiting room so that he could have a word with the woman.

"Your husband's condition is grave," he told her. "If you don't do the following, your husband will surely die":

- Fix him a healthy breakfast every morning, and send him off to work in a good mood.

- When he comes home, let him put his feet up and rest, making sure not to burden him with any worries or household chores.

- Prepare him a warm, nutritious meal for dinner every night.

- Have sex with him several times a week and satisfy his every whim.

On the way home, the wife drove in silence. The husband finally asked, "Well, what did the doctor say?"

"It's bad news," she replied. "He says you're going to die."

I know, that's a terrible joke, but I love it. Why? Because it describes how people often interact with others. They just don't get honest with them. Yet honesty is crucial to credibility. Journalist Edward R. Murrow observed, "To be persuasive we must be believable; to be believable we must be credible; to be credible we must be truthful."

Several years ago, I was speaking to a group of executives, and someone asked me what principles I follow when hiring.

"What's the key?" he asked.

"I have only one rule," I explained. "I never do the hiring." That got their attention. "And here's why: I'm terrible at it."

I went on to explain my horrible track record at hiring people. Because I'm so optimistic and have a high belief in people, I'm unrealistic. It doesn't matter what red flags come up in an interview with a candidate. I always think, *I can help this person to improve and succeed.* That is *not* the right attitude for an interviewer. To be successful in this area, you need people who are skeptical—the kind of individuals who wouldn't even hire their own mothers. When I quit hiring, it took my organization to a whole new level.

When I told this roomful of executives that I didn't do any hiring anymore, I could see their first reaction was negative. But as I explained it, I could sense that they appreciated that I knew my own weaknesses, and they respected my honesty. Few things are worse than someone who doesn't know what he's talking about making things up as he goes along and pretending that he has expertise when he really doesn't have a clue. As blog commenter Roger remarked, "Credibility is not perfection but a willingness to admit imperfection."[6]

BE VULNERABLE

When Bob Garbett was in the Marine Corps, a new second lieutenant fresh out of Officer Candidate School was assigned to his unit. Bob says the young man was obviously overwhelmed by his new assignment. But he handled it well.

"His first day," says Bob, "he called all of the non-commissioned officers together and told us he was counting on us to teach him. He said, 'Don't hurt me. I'm trusting you.' I never forgot his words, and he quickly began to grow into his role in everyone's eyes."[7]

> *"We all know that perfection is a mask. . . . The people with whom we have deepest connection are those who acknowledge their weaknesses."*
>
> —PARKER PALMER

When you are honest with people, it makes you vulnerable. Many people find that to be very uncomfortable. Some leaders, teachers, and speakers believe that someone who communicates to others is supposed to have all the answers. Otherwise, they worry that they will appear weak. But obviously that's an unrealistic standard. It's better to be authentic and vulnerable because people can identify with that, and that leads to connection. Parker Palmer, author of *The Courage to Teach*, says, "We all know that perfection is a mask. So we don't trust the people behind know-it-all masks. They're not being honest with us. The people with whom we have deepest connection are those who acknowledge their weaknesses."

Recently, when talking about leadership to some CEOs, I talked about the importance of being vulnerable, admitting your mistakes, and acknowledging your weaknesses. After I had finished speaking, a CEO waited until I was alone and approached me.

"I think you're totally wrong about being that open with your people," he said. "A leader should never appear weak. You should never let your people see you sweat."

"You know," I responded, "I think you're laboring under a misconception."

"What's that?" he asked skeptically.

"You think your people don't already know your weaknesses," I answered. "They do. By admitting them, you're letting them know that *you* know them."

The reason I told him that with such confidence is that I used to think the way he did. For the first ten years of my career, I tried to be Mr. Answerman. I wanted personally to handle every problem, answer every question, and confront every crisis. I wanted to be indispensable. But I didn't have anybody fooled except myself.

Artist Walter Anderson observed, "Our lives improve only when we take chances—and the first and most difficult risk we can take is to be honest with ourselves." When I realized that others knew things I didn't and could do some things better than I could, it freed me to take off my mask, let down my guard, and be myself with others. And that connects with people. Nobody likes a phony or a know-it-all.

FOLLOW THE GOLDEN RULE

Some organizations are like a tree full of monkeys. If you're a leader at the top of the tree, all you see when you look down is a bunch of smiling faces looking up to you. However, if you're at the bottom of the organization and you look up, the view is not so pretty. And if you stay where you are, you know you're going to get dumped on by everybody who's above you. Nobody wants to be treated that way by others.

Anytime people have power, you can learn a lot about them by watching to see what they do with that power. When they interact with others who don't have power, position, or strength, how do they treat them? Is it consistent with what they communicate? Is it consistent with the Golden Rule? The answer to those questions will tell you a lot about their character.

If you want to connect with others, you need to treat them according to the

> *"Our lives improve only when we take chances—and the first and most difficult risk we can take is to be honest with ourselves."*
>
> —WALTER ANDERSON

241

Golden Rule—you need to treat them as you want to be treated. That's especially true if you are a leader or speaker or you have some other kind of authority. I think most people would agree with that. It's easy to know, but harder to do. As it's been said, wisdom is knowing the right path to take. Integrity is taking it.

One of the leaders I admire is Jim Blanchard, the former CEO of Synovus Financial Corporation, who retired in 2006. Synovus had repeatedly been recognized by *Fortune* as one of the top organizations to work for in the United States. Once when I complimented Jim and asked him the key to the organization's success, he told me, "The company has only one rule—the Golden Rule." He went on to say that in the first two years after it was made known that the Golden Rule would be the standard within Synovus, a third of the executives in the company were fired because they weren't treating people properly. Jim also explained that every year at the company's annual meeting, he used to give out his personal mobile phone number to everyone, telling them if anyone in Synovus treated them in a way that was inconsistent with the Golden Rule, they should call him to tell about it. Now, that's what I call living what you communicate!

DELIVER RESULTS

Peter Drucker, the father of modern management, asserted, "Communication . . . always makes demands. It always demands that the recipient become somebody, do something, believe something. It always appeals to motivation." In other words, communicators exhort people to deliver results. But to be credible as a communicator, you must also deliver results yourself!

I am amazed by the number of speakers, consultants, and life coaches in the marketplace today. Some of them are fantastic, but others have very little credibility. Why? Because they've never actually accomplished anything themselves. They've studied success or leadership or communication, but they've never been on the front lines, building a business, leading an organization, or developing a product or service. They're selling a promise but don't have a track record of success. It mystifies me.

Nothing speaks like results. If you want to build the kind of credibility that connects with people, then deliver results before you deliver a message. Get out and do what you advise others to do. Communicate from experience.

CREDIBILITY CONNECTS

To be successful in the long run, you need to do more than connect. You need to keep connecting, and you can do that only when you live what you communicate. When you do, the results can be fantastic. As I said at the opening of this chapter, the more time goes by, the better the relationship gets.

My friend Collin Sewell, who serves on the board of my nonprofit organization EQUIP, recently told me a story that illustrates the power of living what you communicate. It's no secret how difficult times have been for the American automotive industry. The economy has threatened to put some car manufacturers out of business. Sales are down, incentives are up, and still many dealerships have had to close their doors.

Collin is the CEO of the Sewell Family of Dealerships in Odessa, Texas, so he knows

> *To be successful in the long run, you need to do more than connect. You need to keep connecting, and you can do that only when you live what you communicate.*

firsthand how tough it's been. His family has been in the business of selling cars since 1911, when his grandfather, Carl Sewell Sr, opened a business that was part hardware store, part movie theater, and part Ford dealership. It was soon clear that the Ford dealership was where the potential was. In the nearly one hundred years since, the Sewell family has opened dealerships across Texas to sell and service not only Fords but also vehicles by Cadillac, Hummer, Infiniti, GMC, Lexus, Pontiac, Saab, Buick, Mercury, Lincoln, and Chevrolet. The Sewells have been highly successful.

But going into 2009, times were tough and the businesses were operating in the red. Collin told me that for nine months, he tried everything he could think of to turn it around and get the company back in the black. In March, he even gave himself a 65 percent pay cut, living off of his savings to try to help the business. Nothing seemed to be enough. He finally had to face a difficult decision he was hoping to avoid. Would he lay off many of his employees, or would he cut their salaries?

Many of Collin's advisors shared with him the conventional wisdom: don't cut everyone's salary, because it makes everyone grumpy and it ruins morale. Instead, lay off as many people as you must to make the business profitable. That way the people who are left aren't negatively affected. But Collin didn't want to do that. He wanted to keep the jobs of as many of his people as possible. So he and his management team devised a plan.

They could see no way to avoid cutting twenty jobs, reducing the workforce from 250 to 230. But everyone else—managers, technicians, sales team, and office staff alike—would have to take a cut in pay. The reductions ranged from a dollar an hour in pay up to thousands of dollars in salary.

When Collin announced the pay cuts to the entire staff, he did not expect it to go well—to put it mildly. He told everyone the truth, explaining how dire the situation was, but he figured everyone would still be very angry and negative. One woman, a nine-dollar-per-hour worker who had just received a one-dollar pay cut, approached him after the meeting. He anticipated the worst, but instead of venting, she asked Collin if she could pray with him.

A technician approached Collin, and he could see the anger in the technician's face. "Don't insult me," the technician said. Collin braced himself, expecting to get an earful. But instead the man said, "You didn't cut enough. I'll go home this weekend and talk to my wife, and I'll let you know what my pay should be."

In the end, not one of the employees who took a pay cut quit. Morale remained good. And the business started turning around. How was that possible? Collin had lived what he communicated.

"It took me years to create credibility with my team, to create 'change' with them," Collin says, referring to the idea that you create relational currency in leadership every time you made good decisions and lead with integrity. "I earned that change a nickel and penny at a time. I had to spend it that day by the dollar."

We can't expect to connect with others if we don't live what we communicate. That can hurt someone professionally, but obviously it's even more painful on a personal level. One of the ways I keep myself accountable to live right is to think about the impact of my actions on my family. That's why I always try to keep in mind this definition of success: "Those who are the closest to me and know me the best, love and respect me the most." When the people who know how you live day in, day out, see that your words and actions align, then they can trust you, have confidence in you, and connect with you. And that makes life a great and enjoyable journey every single day.

The true power of connecting with others does not come from superficial interactions with others—smiling at a stranger, being friendly with a food server, or wowing a one-time audience. It comes from connecting with people long-term. In ongoing relationships, we are able to make an impact of real value. When we live with consistent integrity with our spouse, children and grandchildren. When we treat our customers, clients, and colleagues the way they wish to be treated. When our neighbors see our values and actions lining up. When we lead others with honesty and respect. These are the things that give us credibility, allow us to connect, and afford us an opportunity to help others and add value to them. As training consultant Greg Schaffer remarked, "If you do not connect with others, influence is out of the question."[8]

Henry Adams said, "A teacher affects eternity; he can never tell where his influence stops."[9] I believe the same can be said of a connector who has integrity. We can make a difference in our world, but to do so we must begin with ourselves—by making sure our words and our actions are consistent every day. We must live what we communicate. If we do that, there's no telling what we will be able to accomplish.

CONNECTING WITH PEOPLE AT ALL LEVELS

CONNECTING PRACTICE: Connectors live what they communicate.

KEY CONCEPT: The only way to keep connecting with people is to live what you communicate.

CONNECTING ONE-ON-ONE

More than 90 percent of all connecting occurs one-on-one. That's usually how you communicate with the people who know you the best: family, friends, and work associates. You are also least likely to be on your guard with these people and most likely to make commitments to them. As a result, they are the people who know your character best.

Does your character emphasize what you say, or does it undermine it? Does your character help you to follow through and keep your promises, or does it work against you? Where do you need to improve?

CONNECTING IN A GROUP

When we communicate within a group setting or with a team, people look at our example, performance, and teamwork. Are you doing what you ask others to do? Does your track record support your communication? Can people depend on your performance and your willingness to put the team first? If not, you need to make changes to improve your credibility.

CONNECTING WITH AN AUDIENCE

People are most tempted to take character shortcuts when they communicate to an audience because their listeners don't know them personally. It's easy to show only your best side and minimize or entirely cover up your weaknesses. That creates inauthenticity in your communication. People don't connect with communicators who are fakes. Instead, be vulnerable with people and let them know who you really are.

CONCLUSION

People often ask me how I learned leadership and communication. Who were my models? Where did I discover my principles? How have I been able to improve over the years? Certainly I've learned much from watching good leaders and communicators. I've read many great books. I've interviewed leaders who were ahead of me. And I've learned a great deal by trial and error. But the greatest earliest lessons I learned came from the Bible. And I think the story of one of its leaders will be an encouragement to you.

LEARNING TO BE A GREAT CONNECTOR

One of the greatest leaders in human history was Moses. He led an entire nation of people and relocated them and everything they owned from one land to another. He presented them with a code of laws. And he handed the baton to another leader who would settle them in their new home.

But Moses didn't start out as a great leader. If fact, you can see that he had to grow in every area of his life to be successful:

HE WAS NOT GOOD WITH PEOPLE

We think of good leaders and communicators as naturally good with people. That wasn't the case for Moses. In fact, he was so bad with people that in the first recorded incident where he tried to influence another person, an Egyptian, he ended up killing him.[1] Moses had to flee the country and live in exile.

HE WAS NOT A GOOD COMMUNICATOR

When he received God's calling at the burning bush, Moses wanted no part of it. He had no confidence in his ability to communicate with the people. Moses responded, "Who am I, that I should go to Pharaoh and bring the Israelites out of Egypt?"[2] And he added, "O Lord, I have never been eloquent, neither in the past nor since you have spoken to your servant. I am slow of speech and tongue. . . . O Lord, please send someone else to do it."[3] For Moses to accept the assignment, God had to agree to send Moses' brother Aaron with him.

HE WAS NOT A GOOD LEADER

After Moses successfully led the children of Israel out of Egypt, he wasn't particularly successful at leading them farther. The people were continually trying to go in the wrong direction, and Moses was trying to do everything himself—a recipe for failure in leadership. It took Moses' father-in-law, Jethro, to see what he was doing wrong and teach him how to appoint other leaders to help him carry the load.

Why is the example of Moses important? Because it shows that the ability to connect with others, communicate effectively with them, and increase your influence can be learned. Lorin Woolfe, in

The Bible on Leadership, says, "There is a wide-ranging debate about the innateness or 'learnability' of effective communication skills and the nature of 'charisma.'" He weighs in that it can be learned. He wrote,

> God's suggestion to Moses was to team him with his brother Aaron, who was a better speaker. But it was Moses, not Aaron, who spoke to Pharaoh and led his people out of Egypt. What he lacked in speaking ability, Moses possessed in conviction, courage, and compassion for his people. These traits were communicated unmistakably to all who were exposed to him, both follower and foe.

> Moses took what ability he did possess, and he made the most of it. He did what he was called to do, and he increased his influence and used it to help an untold number of people. And he connected with them. When he died, an entire nation wept. The people grieved his loss for thirty days.

START CONNECTING TODAY!

What can you do with the talent you have? Whatever is in you can be put to better use if you learn to connect with people. You can learn to increase your influence in every situation because connecting is more skill than natural talent. And you *can* learn to do it. So start taking steps. Embrace the connecting principles. Start using the connecting practices. And do something positive in your corner of the world.

CONTRIBUTORS TO
JohnMaxwellonLeadership.com

A Maroun, Aaron, Abaunza, Adam Coggin, Adam Henry, Adam Jones, Adam Reineke, Adeyemi Adeleke, Al Fenner, Al Getler, Al White, Alan Humphries, Alana Watkins, Aldo Raharja, Alejandro Pozo, Alessandra Bandeira Malucelli, Alexander Polyakov, Alice McClure, Alisha Callahan, Alison C, Alison Dicken, Alison Gitelson, Allen, Alyssa Lee, Amanda Bouldin, Amanda Kasper, Amanda Strnad, Amenze, Amy King, Amy McCart, Amy Wood, Andrea, Andrew Suryadi, Andy Heller, Andy Perkins, Angela Chrysler, Angela Conrad, Angela Hansen, Angela Mack, Angelina Morris, Ani Victor, Anita Ryan, Annabelle, Anne, Anne Stavrica, Anne-Marie Moutsinga, Anthea, Anthony, Anthony McLean, Anthony T Gitonga, Antoinette Morales, Ardy Roberto, Ariane Ross, Arnold Ardian, B Cassandra Thornton, Babou Srinivasan, Ban Huat, Barb Giglio, Barbie Buckner, Barry Cameron, Bart Looper, Becca, Becca Chen, Becky Laswell, Belinda Hurt, Ben Dawe, Beth Hovekamp, Bethany, Bethany Godwin, Betty, Bev A, Bill Fix, Bill Spinks, Billy Hawkins, Binish, Bob Garbett, Bob Gio, Bob Starkey, Bobbie Nelson, Bobby Capps, Bobby Robson, Bobby Rosa, Brad Cork, Brandon Best, Brandon Byler, Brandon Reed, Brenda Ballard, Brenda McGinnis, Brenton Chomel, Brett Rachel, Brian, Brian Heagle, Brian Jones, Brian Tkatch, Bridget Haymond, Brit, Brittany Turner, Bruce Baker, Bruce Carden, Bryon Ownby, Bud Louse, Buddy, Burdette Rosendale, C Hannan, Caleb Gallifant, Caleb Irmler, Candace Sargent, Carina Dizon, Carl Boniface, Carla Conrad, Carlos Velasquez, Carol Shannon, Carol Shore-Nye, Carolann Jacobs, Carolyn De Jesus, Carolyn Moosvi, Cassandra, Cassie, Cathie Heath, Cathy Kilpatrick, Cathy Welch, Catie Perschke, Catrin Henslee, Chad Payne, Chadwick Wilkerson, Char McAllister, Charlene Hatton, Charles Chung, Charles Coachman, Charles D Martin, Charlie Kentnor, Charlotte, Cheryl, Cheryl Lohner, Cheryl Navaroli, Chew Keng Sheng, Chia Hui Ling, Chike Ekwueme, Chin M C, Christopher B Carrera, Christy Moosa, Chuck Bernal, Chuck Branch, Chut Aleer Deng, Cindy Carreno, Cindy Fisher, Clancy Cross, Clint Neill, Colin Tomlin, Connie Bergeron, Connie Cavender, Connie Martinez, Cora, Craig, Crystal, Curtis, Curtis Howe, Cyndi Toombs, Cynthia

Wesley, Cynthia Zhai, D Jonelle Cousins, D Mann, Dagny Griffin, Daina House, Dale Hart, Dan, Dan Black, Dan Dutrow, Dan Fishbeck, Dan H, Dan Holke, Dana Hayes, Dana Henson, Daniel J Larsen, Daniel Schultz, Daniel Tillman, Daniel Ukpore, Danita Sanders, Danny Anderson, Danny L Smith, Danny Simon, Darrell Irwin, Darren, Darret King, Dave Findlay, Dave Pond, Dave Ramage, Dave Wheeler, Dave Williamson, David Dalka, David Kosberg, David Ligon, David Quach, David Seow, David Seow Sin Khaing, David Tally, Davis B Ochieng, Dawncheri Farrell, Dawnena Rodriguez, Deanne Tillman, Deb, Deb Ingino, Debbie, Debbie Reno, Debora McLaughlin, Debra Steeves, Deeleea, Delbert Ray, Dema Barishnikov, Demetric Phillips, Dennis Chavez, Detra Trueheart, Dewey Esquinance, Dhes Guevarra, Diana Dominguez, Diane, Diane Neff, Diane Stortz, Dominick Stanley, Donna McMeredith, Donna Reavis, Dorina Goetz, Doug Dickerson, Doug Jenkins, Doug Renze, Doug Wilson, Duke Brekhus, Dwayne Hutchings, E J Williams, Earl Waud, Ed Backell, Ed Higgins, Ed Hird, Ed Lopez, Edison Choong, Edith Fragoso de Weyand, Edwin Sarmiento, Elisha Velasco, Elizabeth Ann Yoder, Elizabeth Cottrell, Ellen Bunch, Emily, Emmanuel Eliason, Emran Bhojawala, Ericka Towe, Erin Shell Anthony, Erin Wilcynski, Esele Akhabue, Essy Eisen, Fasanya Adeola, Femi Fortune-Idowu, Folayemi Oyedele, Fradel Barber, Fran, Fran Foreman, Franisz Ginting, Freddy Villareal, Gail McKenzie, Gareth Stead, Gary, Gary Acosta, Gary Haist, Geoffory Anderson, George Dean, George Johnson, George Thimiou, Gerald, Gerald Leonard, Gerald Weathers, Gerry Carrillo, Giaco Higashi, Gilson Cesar Geraldo, Gina Brady, Gloria, Goran Ogar, Grace Bower, Graham, Grant Higgins, Greg Kell, Greg Lubben, Greg Schaffer, Gus, Hank Dagher, Hans Schiefelbein, Heidi Kraft, Helen McCutchen, Henry Will, Henry Yap, Hershel Kreis, Hope Hammond, Htaik Seng, Hydee Miguel VanHook, Intan Jingga, Irfan Simanjuntak, Isabelle Alpert, Ita Imelda, J Bruce Hinton, J Jayson Pagan, J Pinheiro, J R Agosto, J R Davis, Jack Sparling, Jackie Mendez, Jaco Junior, Jacqueline, Jacqueline Campbell, Jacques Fortin, Jake Sledge, James Higginbotham, James M Leath II, James Masimer, James Ost, James Richardson, Jana, Janet Cowan, Janet George, Janine Murray, Jasman Hazly, Jason Glenn, Jason Goss, Jason R Morford, Jason Vreeman, Jasz, Jay Benfield, Jay Stancil, Jeanne Goldman, Jeff Engebose, Jeff Hartley, Jeff Pinkleton, Jenni Baier, Jennie, Jennifer, Jennifer L McCarty, Jennifer Miskov, Jennifer Schwilling, Jennifer Wideman, Jennifer Williams, Jenniffer Vielman-Vasquez, Jeremiah Nyachuru, Jerry Stirpe, Jesse Giglio, Jesse Smith, Jill Beckstedt, Jill Wilberger, Jim Chandler, Jim Ericson, Jim Gore, Jim Johnston, Jim Smith, Jim Thompson, Jimmy Baughcum, Joan Charron, Joanna Holman, Joanna Jayaprakash, Joanne Maly, Jocelyn E Frasier, Jody A Smith, Joe St Germain, Joe Tipton, Joe Windham, Joel Dobbs, Joey Colasito, John Cattani, John Colyer, John Davison, John Gallagher, John Love, John Marker, John O'Donnell, John Sanabria, John See, John Vaprezsan, Johnny Benavides, Johnson Obamehinti, Johnson Tey, Jon M, Jon Rapusas, Jonathan Sutton, Jonell

Hermanson, Jose Franco, Jose M Pujol Hernandez, Joseph DeVenuto, Joseph Garibay, Joseph Marler, Joseph T Duvall, Joseph V Morrone Jr, Joshua Robbins, Joshua Wulf, Joy Holder, Joy Lee, Joyce, Joyce McMurran, Jozel Jerez, Jr Davis, Judy, Judy Camp, Judy Fossgreen, Judy Montgomery, Judy White, Juli Thompson, Julia, Jun S, June Paul, Justin, Justin Joiner, Justin Westcott, Karen, Karen Krogh Christensen, Kasaandra Roache, Katherina H, Kathleen Bankole, Kathy, Kathy Gerstorff, Kathy Nicholls, Kathy Nygaard, Kayode Ejodame, Keith, Keith Brown, Kelley Burns, Ken Anderson, Ken Karpay, Kendra St John, Kent Sanders, Keri Jaehnig, Kerry Atherton, Kevin Beasley, Kevin Card, Kevin Friedman, Kevin Leochko, Kevin Phillips, Kiera Roberto, Kim, Kim Andrews, Kim Kumar, Kimberly Tucker, Krissie Goetz, Kriszel Torres, Kunruthai, Kurt, Kurt Billups, Kyle Prisock, LaCinda, LaFern Batie, Lanny Donoho, Larry Baxter, Larry H, Larry Lanier, Larry Phillips, Lars Ray, Laura Morlando, Laura Nelson, Laura Surovik, Laura Wilkett, Laurie Akau, Laurinda, Laverne, Laverne Lai, Lea Carey, Leann Seehusen, Leonor, Lepang Ferguson, Les Stobbe, Leslie Hulbert, Lew, Lillian Ruiz, Lily Trainor, Linda G Smith, Linda Lister Reinhardt, Lindsay Fawcett, Lindsey Sparks, Lis Maxwell, Lisa Hale, Lisa Kovalchik, Lisa R Combs, Lisa Simmon, Lisa Thorne, Lisa Youngblood, Liza Schwartz, Lois, Lois Mwende, Lokesh S, Lonnie, Lorenzo McGrew, Lori Maas, Lori Mode, Lucas Nel, Lucia Diaz, Lucinda, Luis Fernando Rodriguez Patiño, Lydia Dross, Lydia Maria Gonzalez Dross, Lyn, Lynn Imperiale, M Jason Rump, MacNeal, Madhan, Mai Vu, Malachi O'Brien, Manraj Dhillon, Marc Hopkins, Marc Millan, Marcelo J Paillalef, Marcia, Marcia Neel, Marcos Gaser, Margret Howard, Mariam Bederu, Mariana, Maribeth Hickman, Maribeth Kuzmeski, Marie, Marie Clark, Marie Ruth, Marietjie Steyn, Mariette van Aswegen, Marissa Briones, Mark, Mark Clark, Mark Patrick Brooker, Mark Ralls, Markie Story, Marlene L Balingit, Marshal Ausberry Sr, Martha Castillo, Martha Klein, Martin Gonzalez, Martin Press, Martin Thong, Marvin Penick, Marvin Quianzon, Mary Angelica Reginaldo, Mary Ballard, Mary Martinez, Mary Moh, Mary Toby Ballard, Mary West, MaryAnne, Maryjane Zavala Padron, Maswache, Matt Gaylor, Matthew Mattmiller, Maureen Craig McIntosh, Maureen Sherman, Maurice, Mauro Pennacchia, Mayowa, Mekru Bekele, Melanie Ray, Melissa Albers, Melissa M Frank, Melonie Curry, Metamor4sis, Michael, Michael Barnes, Michael C Tolentino, Michael Craig, Michael Hall, Michael Harrison, Michael Ray, Michael Shuffield, Michelle Pack, Michelle Swallow, Mike Driggers, Mike Henderson, Mike Otis, Mike Parker, Mike Torrey, Mikhaila David, Milton Solorzano, MinistryGeek, Miranda Martin, Miss C, Misty Phillips, Mohnish Bahl, Moises Mendez, Mollie Marti, Monica, Monica Allen, Morten Jacob Sander Andersen, Mr White, Munish Varma, Musho, N C Walker, Nacir Coronado, Nate Manthey, Naw Annabelle, Neil Atiga, Nicholas McDonald, Nicholas Yannacopoulos, Nicole Wyatt, Nigel J Wall, Nina Roach, Nivine Zakhari, Noel Powell, Nona W Kumah, Noni Kaufman, Ogunsakin Adeyemi, Olufunmike Nasiru, Opatola Olufolarin,

P Waterman, Patricia, Patrick L Holder, Patty, Paul, Paul Kandavalli, Paul T, Paulas Panday, Pearlene Harris, People-power, Perry Holley, Pete Krostag, Peter Bishop, Peter G James Sinclair, Peter H, Peter Lee, Peter Nyagah, Petie Huffman, Phil, Phil Holberton, Phil Winn, Philip TFL, Pia, Pinkan Chrisnindia, Piya Medakkar, Polly, Polly Scott, Preston Lawrence, R Burt, R Lynn Lane, R. Moreno, Rachel Bentham, Rachel Setzer, Rachel Shultz, Ralph Guzman, Rambu Elyn Kaborang, Randy Griffin, Raul de la Rosa, Ravi Butalia, Ray McKay Hardee, Raymond Figaro, Raymond Master, Raymond R Brown, Regina Stradford, Rena Williams, Renata Mandia, Rene Jones, Renee Rivera, Renu, Rhonda, Rhonda Baker, Rhonda Thomas, Rhonda York, Richard, Richard Bankert, Richard Boothby, Richard H, Richard Whitehead, Rick, Rick Alanis Jr, Rick Brown, Rick Clack, Rick Costa, Rick Nelson, Rick Pollen, Rick Santiago, Rick Shafer, Ricky, Rita Diba, Robby, Robert Carey, Robert Ferguson, Robert Keen, Robert Nicholson, Robert Zullo, Robin Arnold, Robin Ley, Robin McCoy, Robin Willis, Rodney Stewart, Roger, Rolando Cubero Monge, Ron, Ron Pantoja, Ronnie, Roscoe Thompson, Rosemary Medel, Rowantre, Roy Gibon, Ruben Perez Bustamante, Russell Wright, Rusty Williams, Ruth Demitroff, Ruth Post, Ryan, Ryan Carruthers, Ryan Ladner, Ryan Maraziti, Ryan Tongs, S R Smith, Salman Yazdani, Sam Buchmeyer, Sam McDowell, Samantha, Sandi Benz, Sandie, Sandra Crosson, Sandra Kendell, Sandy Gorman, Sara Canaday, Sarah Doggett, Satinder Manju, Scott A Houchins, Scott Melson, Scott Nichols, Sean Willard, Selma Collier, Septi Suwandi Putra, Shalini, Shantanu Kulkarni, Shari, Shari Berry, Sharon, Sharon Smith, Sharon Tindell, Sharri Tiner, Shawn Ebaugh, Shawn Francis, Shawn Villalovos, Shelley Quiñones, Sheryl, Shiketa, Shiketa Morgan, Shireen, Shirley de Rose, Shyju, Simeone, Simon Herbert, Simone N Riley, Snovia M Slater, Sohail Pirzada, Sohan, Srikrishna, Stacey Lyn Butterfield, Stacey Morgan, Stenovia Curry, Steph, Stephanie, Stephanie Cruz, Stephanie Eagle, Stephany Hanshaw, Steve, Steve McMahan, Steve Payne, Steven Hiscoe, Subu Musti, Sue Cartun, Sue Duffield, Sumesh, Sun Yi Scott, Sunnie Templeton, Susan Davis, Susan Wright-Boucher, Suuprmansd, Suzanne Caldeira, T, Tamella Davies, Tami Rush, Tammie Dobson, Tanja van Zyl, Tara Lancaster, Tara Turkington, Ted Oatts, Teresita Vigan, Teri Aulph, Terri Trapp, Terry, Terry D Smith, Terry McReath, Terry Smith, Tes Casin, Theresia Halim, Thomas Kinsfather, Thomas Nyaruwata, Thomas Watson, Tiffany Wright, Tim Buttrey, Tim Skinner, Timothy, Timothy Teasdale, TJ Ermitaño, Tobi Lytle, Tochi, Tom Chereck Jr, Tom Cocklereece, Tom Martin, Tom McCrea, Tony L Jones, Tracy Hunter, Tran Bao Hung, Trudy Metzger, Twyla Allen, Val, Vera L E Archilla, Vicki, Vicki Znavor, Vickie, Vixon, VoNi Deon, Vskumar, W Dwight Kelly, Wade Sadlier, Wade Thompson, Waldemar Smit, Walt Kean, Wanda, Warren Blake, Wendi Weir, Wennie Comision, William Eickhoff, Wylie Rhinehart Jr, Yousuf Siddiqui, Yvette Kinley, Yvonne Green, Zeina.

Notes

CHAPTER 1

1. "Welcome to the Age of Communications," Elway Research, Inc., http://www.elwayresearch.com, accessed 21 October 2008.
2. Matthias R. Mehl et al, "Are Women Really More Talkative Than Men?" *Science*, 6 July 2007, 82, http://www.sciencemag.org/cgi/content/full/317/5834/82, accessed 11 November 2008.
3. Quoted in G. Michael Campbell, *Bulletproof Presentations* (Franklin Lakes, NJ: Career Press, 2002), 7.
4. John Baldoni, *Great Communication Secrets of Great Leaders* (New York: McGraw-Hill, 2003), xv–xvi.
5. Bert Decker, "The Top Ten Best (and Worst) Communicators of 2008," Decker Blog, http://www.bertdecker.com/experience/2008/12/top-ten-best-and-worst-communicators-of-2008.html, accessed 6 January 2009.
6. Tom Martin, blog comment, 10 September 2009, http://johnmaxwellonleadership.com/2009/08/31/connecting-increases-your-influence-in-every-situation/#comments.
7. Cassandra Washington, blog comment, 13 September 2009, http://johnmaxwellonleadership.com/2009/08/31/connecting-increases-your-influence-in-every-situation/#comments.
8. Lindsay Fawcett, blog comment, 1 September 2009, http://johnmaxwellonleadership.com/2009/08/31/connecting-increases-your-influence-in-every-situation/#comments.
9. Jennifer Williams, 31 August 2009, http://johnmaxwellonleadership.com/2009/08/31/connecting-increases-your-influence-in-every-situation/#comments.
10. Al Getler, 10 September 2009, http://johnmaxwellonleadership.com/2009/08/31/connecting-increases-your-influence-in-every-situation/#comments.
11. Jay Hall, "To Achieve or Not: The Manager's Choice," Adapted from *California Management Review*, vol. 18, no. 4, 5–18, http://theraffettogroup.com/To%20Achieve%20or%20Not.pdf, accessed 21 September 2009.

12. Cathy Welch, 1 September 2009, http://johnmaxwellonleadership.com/2009/08/31/connecting-increases-your-influence-in-every-situation/#comments.

CHAPTER 2

1. Isabelle Alpert, blog comment, 14 September 2009, http://johnmaxwellonleadership.com/2009/09/13/connecting-is-all-about-others/#comments.
2. Barb Giglio, blog comment, 14 September 2009, http://johnmaxwellonleadership.com/2009/09/13/connecting-is-all-about-others/#comments.
3. Gail McKenzie, blog comment, 14 September 2009, http://johnmaxwellonleadership.com/2009/09/13/connecting-is-all-about-others/#comments.
4. Joel Dobbs, blog comment, 15 September 2009, http://johnmaxwellonleadership.com/2009/09/13/connecting-is-all-about-others/#comments.
5. Pete Krostag, blog comment, 20 September 2009, http://johnmaxwellonleadership.com/2009/09/13/connecting-is-all-about-others/#comments.
6. Michael V. Hernandez, "Restating Implied, Perspective and Statutory Easements," *Real Property, Probate and Trust Journal* (American Bar Association, Spring 2005), cited in *May It Please the Court,* http://www.mayitpleasethecourt.com/journal.asp?blogID=898, accessed 20 November 2008.
7. Calvin Miller, *The Empowered Communicator: 7 Keys to Unlocking an Audience* (Nashville: Broadman & Holman, 1994), 42.
8. Attributed to Joann C. Jones, *All Great Quotes,* http://www.allgreatquotes.com/graduation_quotes.shtml, accessed 8 December 2008.
9. Bridget Haymond, blog comment, 15 September 2009, http://johnmaxwellonleadership.com/2009/09/13/connecting-is-all-about-others/#comments.
10. Chew Keng Sheng, blog comment, 19 September 2009, http://johnmaxwellonleadership.com/2009/09/13/connecting-is-all-about-others/#comments.
11. "Peter Irvine and Nabi Saleh: The Glory of the Bean," *Wealth Creator,* January/February 2006, http://www.wealthcreator.com.au/peter-irvine-nabi-saleh-gloria-jeans.html, accessed 5 January 2009.
12. Ibid.
13. "Lessons from Top Entrepreneurs: Cup of Re-charge Juice," *Smart Company,* 8 January 2008, http://www.smartcompany.com.au/Features/Lessons-from-Top-Entrepreneurs/20071211-Cup-of-re-charge-juice.html, accessed 5 January 2009.
14. "Gloria Jean's Coffees International," Gloria Jean's Coffees, http://www.gloriajeanscoffees.com.au/pages/content.asp?pid=77, accessed 13 January 2009.
15. "Peter Irvine and Nabi Saleh: The Glory of the Bean," *Wealth Creator,* January/ February 2006, http://www.wealthcreator.com.au/peter-irvine-nabi-saleh-gloria-jeans.htm, accessed 5 January 2009.

16. Laura Surovik, blog comment, 18 September 2009, http://johnmaxwell onleadership.com/2009/09/13/connecting-is-all-about-others/#comments.

17. Calvin Miller, *The Empowered Communicator* (Nashville: Broadman & Holman, 1994), 12.

18. Jerry Weissman, *Presenting to Win: The Art of Telling Your Story* (Upper Saddle River, NJ: FT Press, 2008), 7.

19. Emran Bhojawala, blog comment, 16 September 2009, http://johnmaxwell onleadership.com/2009/09/13/connecting-is-all-about-others/#comments.

20. Mike Otis, blog comment, 20 September 2009, http://johnmaxwellon leadership.com/2009/09/13/connecting-is-all-about-others/#comments.

CHAPTER 3

1. "Silent Messages—A Wealth of Information About Nonverbal Communication (BodyLanguage)". http://www.kaaj.com/psych/smorder.html, accessed 16 December 2008.

2. Sonya Hamlin, *How to Talk So People Listen* (New York: Collins Business, 2005), 59.

3. Ibid., 11.

4. John Love, blog comment, 21 September 2009, http://johnmaxwellon leadership.com/2009/09/20/connecting-goes-beyond-words/#comments.

5. Sue Duffield, blog comment, 27 September 2009, http://johnmaxwellon leadership.com/2009/09/20/connecting-goes-beyond-words/#comments.

6. Source unknown.

7. Steven Hiscoe, blog comment, 21 September 2009, http://johnmaxwellon leadership.com/2009/09/20/connecting-goes-beyond-words/#comments.

8. Hershel Kreis, blog comment, 22 September 2009, http://johnmaxwellon leadership.com/2009/09/20/connecting-goes-beyond-words/#comments.

9. J. Jayson Pagan, blog comment, 23 September 2009, http://johnmaxwell onleadership.com/2009/09/20/connecting-goes-beyond-words/#comments.

CHAPTER 4

1. Susan RoAne, "Chapter Four: Visibility Value," www.susanroane.com/books _tapes/booksecretschap4.html, accessed 19 January 2010.

2. Laurinda Bellinger, blog comment, 4 October 2009, http://johnmaxwell onleadership.com/2009/09/27/connecting-always-requires-energy/ #comments.

3. Simon Herbert, blog comment, 28 September 2009, http://johnmaxwell onleadership.com/2009/09/27/connecting-always-requires-energy/ #comments.

4. Lisa Thorne, blog comment, 28 September 2009, http://johnmaxwellon leadership.com/2009/09/27/connecting-always-requires-energy/#comments.

5. Trudy Metzger, blog comment, 28 September 2009, http://johnmaxwell

onleadership.com/2009/09/27/connecting-always-requires-energy/
#comments.

6. Ed Higgins, blog comment, 4 October 2009, http://johnmaxwellonleader
    ship.com/2009/09/27/connecting-always-require-energy/#comments.

7. José Manuel Pujol Hernández, blog comment, 3 October 2009, http://
    johnmaxwellonleadership.com/2009/09/27/connecting-always-requires
    -energy/#comments.

8. Anne Cooper Ready, *Off the Cuff: What to Say at a Moment's Notice* (Franklin
    Lakes, NJ: Career Press, 2004), 19.

9. Ryan Schleisman, blog comment, 29 September 2009, http://johnmaxwell
    onleadership.com/2009/09/27/connecting-always-requires-energy/
    #comments.

10. Clancy Cross, blog comment, 3 October 2009, http://johnmaxwellonlead
    ership.com/2009/09/27/connecting-always-requires-energy/#comments.

CHAPTER 5

1. Lars Ray, blog comment, 5 October 2009, http://johnmaxwellonleader
    ship.com/2009/10/04/connecting-is-more-skill-than-natural-talent/
    #comments.

2. Jesse Giglio, blog comment, 8 October 2009, http://johnmaxwellonleader
    ship.com/2009/10/04/connecting-is-more-skill-than-natural-talent/
    #comments.

3. "The Evolution of George Michael" by Imaeyen Ibanga [Interview with
    Chris Cuomo], *Good Morning America*, 24 July 2008, http://abcnews.go
    .com/GMA/SummerConcert/story?id=5432454&page=1.

CHAPTER 6

1. Adapted from the *Saturday Evening Post*, May/June 2006, 6.

2. Terry Felber, *Am I Making Myself Clear? Secrets of the World's Greatest
    Communicators* (Nashville: Thomas Nelson, 2002), 118–20.

3. Submitted by John Ross, *Leadership*, Spring 1991.

4. Deb Ingino, blog comment, 18 October 2009, http://johnmaxwellonlead
    ership.com/2009/10/11/connectors-connect-on-common-ground/
    #comments.

5. Quoted by Franisz Ginging, blog comment, 16 October 2009, http://john
    maxwellonleadership.com/2009/10/11/connectors-connect-on-common
    -ground/#comments.

6. D. Michael Abrashoff, *It's Your Ship* (New York: Warner Books, 2002), 55.

7. C. Hannan, blog comment, 18 October 2009, http://johnmaxwellonlead
    ership.com/2009/10/11/connectors-connect-on-common-ground/
    #comments.

8. Jim Lundy, *Lead, Follow, or Get out of the Way* (New York: Berkley Books, 1986), 5.

9. Ibid, 50.

10. Hans Schiefelbein, blog comment, 18 October 2009, http://johnmaxwell onleadership.com/2009/10/11/connectors-connect-on-common -ground/#comments.

11. Duke Brekhus, blog comment, 14 October 2009, http://johnmaxwellon leadership.com/2009/10/11/connectors-connect-on-common -ground/#comments.

12. *Webster's New World Dictionary of American English,* Third College Edition (New York: Webster's New World, 1991).

13. Michelle Pack, blog comment, 13 October 2009, http://johnmaxwellon leadership.com/2009/10/11/connectors-connect-on-common-ground/ #comments.

14. Grace Bower, personal e-mail, 21 October 2009.

15. Quoted in Pat Williams, *American Scandal* (Treasure House, 2003), 230–31.

16. Joel Dobbs, blog comment, 17 October 2009, http://johnmaxwellonleader ship.com/2009/10/11/connectors-connect-on-common-ground/#comments.

CHAPTER 7

1. Ronnie Ding, blog comment, 19 October 2009, http://johnmaxwellon leadership.com/2009/10/18/connectors-do-the-difficult-work-of-keeping -it-simple/#comments.

2. Sue Cartun, blog comment, 19 October 2009, http://johnmaxwellon leadership.com/2009/10/18/connectors-do-the-difficult-work-of-keeping -it-simple/#comments.

3. "Engrish? Bad English Translations on International Signs," http://www .joe-ks.com/Engrish.htm, accessed 16 March 2009.

4. Janet George, blog comment, 25 October 2009, http://johnmaxwellon leadership.com/2009/10/18/connectors-do-the-difficult-work-of keeping- it-simple/#comments.

5. *Harvard Business Review,* 1989.

6. Ann Cooper Ready, *Off the Cuff* (Franklin Lakes, NJ: Career Press, 2004), 66.

CHAPTER 8

1. Lars Ray, blog comment, 26 October 2009, http://johnmaxwellonleadership. com/2009/10/26/connectors-create-an-experience-everyone-enjoys/ #comments.

2. Joseph Marler, blog comment, 26 October 2009, http://johnmaxwellon leadership.com/2009/10/26/connectors-create-an-experience-everyone -enjoys/#comments.

3. Robert Keen, blog comment, 26 October 2009, http://johnmaxwellon leadership.com/2009/10/26/connectors-create-an-experience-everyone -enjoys/#comments.

4. Jeff Roberts, blog comment, 1 November 2009, http://johnmaxwellon leadership.com/2009/10/26/connectors-create-an-experience-everyone -enjoys/#comments.
5. Proverbs 17:22 NIV.
6. Nancy Beach, *Celebration of Hope*, Part 1, Willow Creek Resources, 4/20/ 2008.
7. Duke Brekhus, blog comment, 27 October 2009, http://johnmaxwellon leadership.com/2009/10/26/connectors-create-an-experience-everyone -enjoys/#comments.
8. Candace Sargent, blog comment, 1 November 2009, 27 October 2009, http://johnmaxwellonleadership.com/2009/10/26/connectors-create -an-experience-everyone-enjoys/#comments.
9. Billy Hawkins, blog comment, 30 October 2009, 27 October 2009, http:// johnmaxwellonleadership.com/2009/10/26/connectors-create-an -experience-everyone-enjoys/#comments.

CHAPTER 9

1. *NY Journal-American* 9 Mar 1954, quoted in Simpson's Contemporary Quotations, compiled by James B. Simpson. 1988, Bartleby.com, http:// www.bartleby.com/63/34/4634.html, accessed 30 March 2009.
2. Lea Carey, blog comment, 8 November 2009, http://johnmaxwellonlead ership.com/2009/11/02/connectors-inspire-people/#comments.
3. Adam Henry, blog comment, 5 November 2009, http://johnmaxwellon leadership.com/2009/11/02/connectors-inspire-people/#comments.
4. Jacques Fortin, blog comment, 5 November 2009, http://johnmaxwellon leadership.com/2009/11/02/connectors-inspire-people/#comments.
5. Bart Looper, blog comment, 6 November 2009, http://johnmaxwellon leadership.com/2009/11/02/connectors-inspire-people/#comments.
6. Doug Wilson, blog comment, 2 November 2009, http://johnmaxwellon leadership.com/2009/11/02/connectors-inspire-people/#comments.
7. Larry Phillips, blog comment, 3 November 2009, http://johnmaxwellon leadership.com/2009/11/02/connectors-inspire-people/#comments.
8. Brad Cork, blog comment, 2 November 2009, http://johnmaxwellonlead ership.com/2009/11/02/connectors-inspire-people/#comments.
9. Joyce McMurran, blog comment, 8 November 2009, http://johnmaxwell onleadership.com/2009/11/02/connectors-inspire-people/#comments.
10. Jerry Weissman, *Presenting to Win: The Art of Telling Your Story*, updated and Expanded Edition (Upper Saddle River, NJ: Financial Times Press, 2009), xxvi–xxvii.
11. Maribeth Hickman, blog comment, 5 November 2009, http://johnmaxwell onleadership.com/2009/11/02/connectors-inspire-people/#comments.
12. Raymond Master, blog comment, 8 November 2009, http://johnmaxwell onleadership.com/2009/11/02/connectors-inspire-people/#comments.

CHAPTER 10

1. Carl M. Cannon, "Ten Reasons Why Obama Won," Reader'sDigest.com, 5 November 2008, http://www.rd.com/blogs/loose-cannon/ten-reasons-why -obama-won/post7386.html, accessed 3 April 2009.

2. Brett Rachel, blog comment, 15 November 2009, http://johnmaxwellon leadership.com/2009/11/09/connectors-live-what-they-communicate/ #comments.

3. Ray McKay Hardee, blog comment, 15 November 2009, http://johnmaxwell onleadership.com/2009/11/09/connectors-live-what-they-communicate/ #comments.

4. Lindsay Fawcett, blog comment, 15 November 2009, http://johnmaxwell onleadership.com/2009/11/09/connectors-live-what-they-communicate/ #comments.

5. Adam Jones, blog comment, 9 November 2009, http://johnmaxwellon leadership.com/2009/11/09/connectors-live-what-they-communicate/ #comments.

6. Roger, blog comment, 15 November 2009, http://johnmaxwellonleadership .com/2009/11/09/connectors-live-what-they-communicate/#comments.

7. Bob Garbett, blog comment, 9 November 2009, http://johnmaxwellon- leadership.com/2009/11/09/connectors-live-what-they-communicate/ #comments.

8. Greg Schaffer, blog comment, 8 November 2009, http://johnmaxwellon leadership.com/2009/11/02/connectors-inspire-people/#comments.

9. Bethany Godwin, blog comment, 15 November 2009, http://johnmaxwell onleadership.com/2009/11/09/connectors-live-what-they-communicate/ #comments.

CONCLUSION

1. Exodus 2:11–14.

2. Exodus 3:11 NIV.

3. Exodus 4:10, 13 NIV.

ABOUT THE AUTHOR

John C. Maxwell is an internationally respected leadership expert, speaker, and author who has sold more than 18 million books. Dr. Maxwell is the founder of EQUIP, a non-profit organization that has trained more than 5 million leaders in 126 countries worldwide. Each year he speaks to the leaders of diverse organizations, such as Fortune 500 companies, foreign governments, the National Football League, the United States Military Academy at West Point, and the United Nations. A *New York Times*, *Wall Street Journal*, and *Business Week* best-selling author, Maxwell has written three books that have sold more than a million copies: *The 21 Irrefutable Laws of Leadership*, *Developing the Leader Within You*, and *The 21 Indispensable Qualities of a Leader*. His blog can be read at JohnMaxwellonLeadership.com.

BOOKS BY DR. JOHN C. MAXWELL
CAN TEACH YOU HOW TO BE A REAL SUCCESS

RELATIONSHIPS

Everyone Communicates, Few Connect
Encouragement Changes Everything
25 Ways to Win With People
Winning With People
Relationships 101
The Treasure of a Friend
The Power of Partnership in the Church
Becoming a Person of Influence
Be A People Person
The Power of Influence
Ethics 101

ATTITUDE

Self-Improvement 101
Success 101
The Difference Maker
How Successful People Think
The Journey From Success to Significance
Attitude 101
Failing Forward
Your Bridge to a Better Future
Living at the Next Level
The Winning Attitude
Be All You Can Be
The Power of Thinking Big
Think on These Things
The Power of Attitude
Thinking for a Change

EQUIPPING

Teamwork 101
My Dream Map
Put Your Dream to the Test
Make Today Count
The Choice Is Yours
Mentoring 101
Talent is Never Enough
Equipping 101
Developing the Leaders Around You
The 17 Essential Qualities of a Team Player
Success One Day at a Time
The 17 Indisputable Laws of Teamwork
Your Road Map for Success
Today Matters
Partners in Prayer

LEADERSHIP

Leadership Promises For Your Work Week
Leadership Gold
Go for Gold
The 21 Most Powerful Minutes
in a Leader's Day
Revised & Updated 10th Anniversary
Edition of *The 21 Irrefutable*
Laws of Leadership
The 360 Degree Leader
Leadership Promises for Every Day
Leadership 101
The Right to Lead
The 21 Indispensable Qualities of a Leader
Developing the Leader Within You
The Power of Leadership

DON'T LEAVE YOUR DREAM TO CHANCE

IT'S ONE THING TO DREAM ABOUT YOUR PERFECT FUTURE. ANOTHER TO ACHIEVE IT.

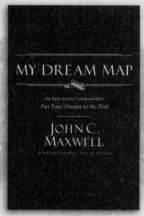

In *Put Your Dream to the Test* John Maxwell brings the subject of a dream down to earth and provides a step by-step action plan you can start using today to see, own, and reach your dream.

A complement to *Put Your Dream to the Test, My Dream Map* leads readers through the process of clarifying their dream and finding the path to achieve it.

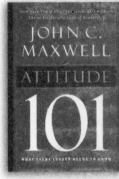
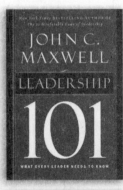
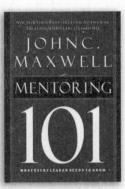
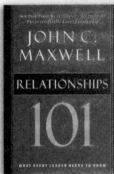

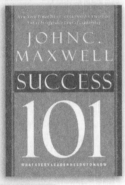

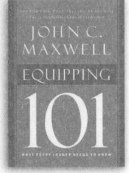

LEADERSHIP.

IT ALL BEGINS WITH GOD,
THE ULTIMATE LEADER.

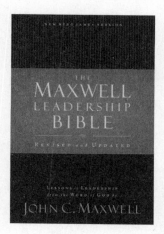

From Genesis to Revelation, the people, events, and teachings of the Bible are God's treasury of wisdom and guidance for anyone who has been called to be a person of influence. Whether you're an executive, a pastor, an entrepreneur, a parent, a coach, or a teacher, you are a leader, someone who influences and encourages others on a daily basis.

John C. Maxwell brings the laws of leadership to a new level in this revised and updated briefcase edition of *The Maxwell Leadership Bible*. Dr. Maxwell walks you through the New King James Bible text as he draws from his decades of godly leadership and best-selling resources to illuminate the time-tested and life-changing principles of leadership in Scripture. Now available in a new easy to carry size, this Bible is the ideal gift for every leader striving to be extraordinary.